Autonomous Media
ACTIVATING RESISTANCE AND DISSENT

copyleft ø 2005 Andrea Langlois + Frédéric Dubois
copyleft ø 2005 Cumulus Press

copyleft : may be reproduced in its entirety (as a complete work) with prior written consent of the publisher or editors, provided it is distributed and provided to the reader for free, without service charges or any other fee. Each essay, illustration, photograph, endeavour herein is the property of its respective creator.

Dépôt légal, Bibliothèque nationale du Québec, 2e trimestre 2005
Legal deposit, National Library of Canada, 2nd quarter 2005

Library and Archives Canada Cataloguing in Publication

    Autonomous media : activating resistance and dissent / edited by Andrea Langlois, Frédéric Dubois.

Includes bibliographical references.
ISBN 0-9733499-4-8

    1. Alternative mass media. 2. Social movements.
I. Langlois, Andrea II. Dubois, Frédéric

HM1206.M37 2005   302.23   C2005-902004-0

designed and typeset by Chester Rhoder @ Typo-Pawsitive

photographs:
Bernard Bastien (pgs. 8, 39, 49, 51, 52, 58, 105, 108, 150)
Clara Gabriel (pgs. 54, 56, 59)
L'Itinéraire (pgs. 92, 95, 101)
Stéphane Lahoud (pg. 73)
Dawn Paley (pgs. 7, 21, 28, 29, 97, 111, 119)
Chester Rhoder (pgs. 40, 45, 57, 126, 131, 136, 143, 146)
Andréa Schmidt (pgs. 80, 83, 86, 87)
Andrew Stern (pgs. 79, 84, 85)

illustrations:
Fanchon Esquieu (pgs. 5, 18, 19, 20, 21, 22, 23, 25, 32, 33, 35, 37, 55, 98, 112, 138, 144)
Élise Gravel (pgs. 16, 30, 46, 60, 74, 88, 102, 122, 134)
Pink Panthers Collective, Montréal (pg. 62)
Public Works Collective (pgs. 65, 66, 68, 69)
Jesse Purcell & Marielle Levine (pg. 106)
Chester Rhoder (pgs. 3, 7, 70, 116)

Cumulus Press
P.O. Box 5205, Station B
Montréal (Québec)
Canada H3B 4B5
www.cumuluspress.com

Printed by
Imprimerie Gauvin in Gatineau, Québec
on **100% post-consumer recycled paper**.

Cumulus Press acknowledges the support of the Canada Council for the Arts for its publishing program.

Canada Council for the Arts   Conseil des Arts du Canada

To all those with the audacity
to seize the media.

Ce recueil de textes est dédié aux petits monstres qui,
au quotidien, nous donnent le goût de continuer.
Nous pensons particulièrement à
Ali, Anäel, Esteban, Forest, Ilan, Julienne,
Kaili, Malcolm, River, Véïa, et Zach.

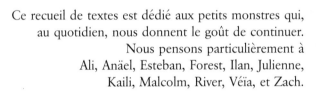

9		introduction
		BY ANDREA LANGLOIS & FRÉDÉRIC DUBOIS
17	one	hard at work in the bamboo garden
		MEDIA ACTIVISTS AND SOCIAL MOVEMENTS
		BY SCOTT UZELMAN
31	two	broadcasting on our own terms
		TEMPORARY AUTONOMOUS RADIO
		BY MARIAN VAN DER ZON
47	three	how open is open?
		THE POLITICS OF OPEN PUBLISHING
		BY ANDREA LANGLOIS
61	four	101 tricks to play with the mainstream
		CULTURE JAMMING AS SUBVERSIVE RECREATION
		BY TOM LIACAS
75	five	independent reporting
		A TOOL FOR INTERNATIONAL SOLIDARITY BUILDING
		BY ANDRÉA SCHMIDT
89	six	echoes from the curb
		STREET NEWSPAPERS AND EMPOWERMENT
		BY ISABELLE MAILLOUX-BÉÏQUE
103	seven	screening the revolution
		FAQs ABOUT VIDEO ACTIVISM
		BY DAVID WIDGINGTON
123	eight	re/writing media
		WEBLOGS AS AUTONOMOUS SPACES
		BY DAWN PALEY
135	nine	networkers unite!
		STRENGTHENING MEDIA SOLIDARITY
		BY FRÉDÉRIC DUBOIS
151		afterword
		LINKING BACK, LOOKING FORWARD
		BY DOROTHY KIDD
162		bibliography
165		contributors
168		acknowledgements

"in crisis, subversion"

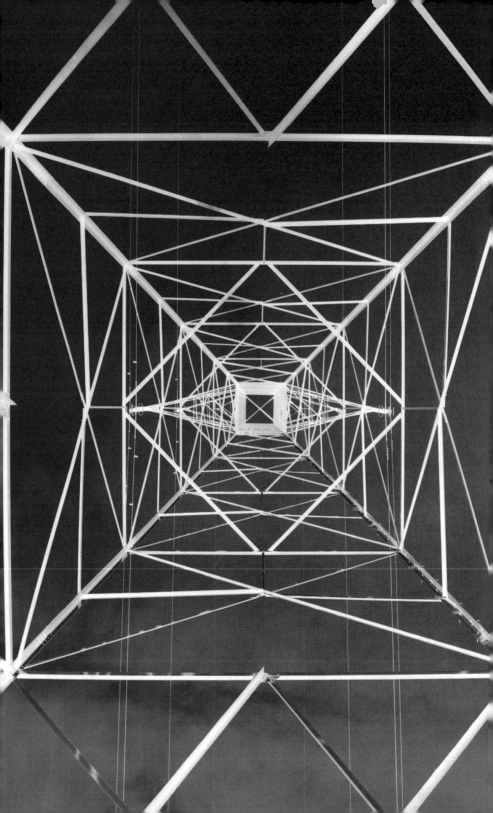

introduction
by andrea langlois & frédéric dubois

Autonomous media are the vehicles of social movements. They are attempts to subvert the social order by reclaiming the means of communication. What defines these media, and makes them a specific type of alternative media, is that they, first and foremost, undertake to amplify the voices of people and groups normally without access to media. They seek to work autonomously from dominant institutions (e.g. the state, corporations, the church, the military, corporatist unions), and they encourage the participation of audiences within their projects. Autonomous media therefore produce communication that is not one-way, from media-makers to media consumers, but instead involves the bilateral participation of people as producers and recipients of information.

The content of autonomous media is intended to provide information that supports social struggles and is alternative to that which is offered by the corporate mass media. True alternative discourses can only be fostered through a media organization that remains open, transparent, and non-hierarchical. For that reason, autonomous media move beyond the issues of content and into those of organization, participation, and empowerment.

Autonomous media, ranging from pamphlets to newspapers, pirate radio to websites, are increasingly part of the activist toolkit. They are the spaces into which the rationales and analyses of activists are launched, with the hope that seeds will be sown to help movements grow, ripen, and bear the fruit of social change. Media is society's resource for self-representation but the world can not be changed merely through the images and words presented in the media. True change will come only through people's participation in the processes of social change.

The goal of media activists is not to replace mainstream media with a new form of media monopoly, but instead to contest the symbolic reality constructed by corporate institutions of media concentration. As Patrick Cadorette, media activist, words it, "Today, through their generic control of the global mediascape, highly concentrated financial interests have achieved unprecedented influence over the way we think, see, and shape the world. We now depend on transnational corporations, banks, insurance companies, arms-makers and traders to seek, receive, and impart information and ideas on our behalf."[1]

Media activists seek not only to provide a space for information that is an alternative to that which is found in mass media, but also to create media that breakdown hierarchies of access to meaning-making, therefore allowing those typically found at the grassroots to have a voice and to define reality. Feminists have been addressing this question for the past 30 years, arguing against positivistic discourses that divide knowledge into the rational (legitimate and objective) and the irrational (illegitimate and subjective). Yet the problem remains that some segments of the population have more power to "speak truth" than others and that radical discourses are naturalized and thus neutralized.

Although there are gaps within the mass media in which radical discourses sometimes take hold, the overall picture shows a mediascape in which certain voices are privileged and in which dissent is used to reinforce the status quo. As Scott Uzelman illustrates in chapter one, media activists view the corporate media machine as a formidable obstacle to social movements. Corporate media structures both support and benefit from capitalism—they are businesses bent on making a profit, not on challenging the status quo. Mainstream media reinforce political apathy and discourage political engagement. Media convergence and the concentration of media have led to the homogenization of information, not to its diversification, thus widening the divide between those with discursive legitimacy—i.e., the right to speak and be heard—and those without.

If the global justice movement is committed to changing the world, its participants must struggle to reclaim and to create spaces in which all people can participate in communication and culture, and therefore in politics. Media and public communication are important tools for the growth and survival of social movements, tools which are not just about socio-economics, but also, and perhaps primarily, about access to systems of meaning-making.[2] Activists from all social movements must therefore work towards the democratization of media and must also seize the media themselves.

The idea of seizing the media is not new in Canada. Social movement activists have always created and used various forms of media to get their message across. In the beginning of the 19th century, pamphlets were all the rage, as were politically-oriented newspapers. Later, with the advent of the common office photocopier came an outpouring of self-published 'zines, flyers, and chapbooks. In the 1980s, the anarchist community was mastering the low-tech art of self-publishing, with publications, like British Columbia's BLACKOUT and Toronto's ECOMEDIA, helping to spread news and ideas.[3] The technology of fax machines brought autonomous media to a new level, making it easier for activists to share information with each other over vast distances.

Also over the past twenty or thirty years, Indigenous filmmakers in Canada—such as Alanis Obomsawin and Christine Welsh—have reclaimed a tool that has served an important role in colonization—the camera—using film as a way to resist colonization and to expose the oppression of Indigenous peoples in Canada. As documented in the essays by Marian van der Zon (chapter two) and David Widgington (chapter seven), the rise of cheaper and more accessible video and radio technologies have led to an increase in the amount of activist film and radio in grassroots movements. The internet has brought with it its own advantages, such as fast and easy communication through email and easy self-publishing, as illustrated in the essays on Indymedia and weblogging by Andrea Langlois (chapter three) and Dawn Paley (chapter eight), respectively.

The aim of this collection of essays is to document some of the practices of today's media activists—their strategies, tactics, challenges, and successes. It is not simply an academic communications reader, nor is it an activist toolbox—it is both and much more. We began this project after noticing that little documentation and discussion on autonomous media exists, even though knowledge and analysis around it abounds within activist communities. The purpose of this book is therefore to harness this knowledge and to create a space within which to discuss and explore autonomous media tactics developed within a Canadian context. By shinning a spotlight on these marginal media projects, we hope to draw people towards them—like butterflies to a light-bulb—to experience, first-hand, the power of organizing autonomously and producing media.

This book is about media that blossom out of the repetitive efforts of ordinary people who are fed-up with the mainstream media. It is about those who decide to act in favour of the long march towards media democracy. This collective effort has been made possible by the contributions of devoted people who view the mediascape as a battlefield. This field of confrontation between commercial-, social movement-, and state-driven logics[4] is, in the heads of media activists, one of the determining foundations upon which capitalism regenerates itself and spreads injustice. This is why they act. This is why they write. This is why they have chosen to collaborate in this project, to share their experiences and analysis around autonomous media. They are a part of the social movements they describe. They are media activists.

Each chapter was written to stand alone, so the reader can approach the book in the order she or he wishes. Yet, there are several fundamentals which permeate the entire book. To begin with, connections between media that are temporary or permanent—media set up to cover a one-week protest, or established community radio, respectively—are addressed by each author. Some autonomous media are put together by ad-hoc coalitions, whereas others are planned with care and last for years. This is an aspect discussed in each chapter of the book, and which is especially important in a context where the need for projects that support resistance and dissent come and go. The temporary versus permanent, but more importantly the combination of both in the form of tactics and strategies are emphasized.

Also transversal to the book is the global aspect of current social movements. All authors address the dynamics of global and local struggles in which autonomous media are embedded and to which they contribute ammunition. Although many of the writers are based in Montréal, they have all made an effort to draw on examples from other cities and countries. They examine the local, regional, national, and international implications of the autonomous media they describe and analyze.

These themes help situate autonomous media within an increasingly globalized world, which is ever-changing, and thus creating openings, limitations, and opportunities for media activists. Some authors—such as Andréa Schmidt (chapter five) and Isabelle Mailloux-Béique (chapter six)—also describe specific autonomous media projects. They discuss them within a perspective of social change and the empowerment of communities participating in, and affected by, these projects. In addition to exploring the broadcasting, screening, and publishing of content created by and for activists and marginalized groups, they tackle issues such as the role of media activists in social movements (chapters one and five), the relationships among media projects (chapter nine), and the organizational aspects of autonomous media (chapter six, seven, and nine).

The book begins with an exploratory chapter on media activism, in which Uzelman theorizes why communication is so important to social movement networks. It then goes on to examine the tactics and strategies of people who take up communication-centred struggles. The following chapters delve into more specific examples, inviting the reader to explore various media from activist video (chapter seven), to culture jamming (chapter four), to street newspapers (chapter six), along with computer-mediated tools such as open publishing, as practiced within Indymedia (chapter three), and weblogs (chapter eight). These essays provide the reader with a sense of the plurality and diversity of autonomous media projects, illuminating the importance and roles of autonomous media within their communities and publics. Other essays address the larger issues around autonomous media, such as independent reporting as a tool for international solidarity-building (chapter five) and the importance of building autonomous media networks (chapter nine). In the afterword, Dorothy Kidd, a seasoned media activist and academic, reflects back on the book, providing some historical context for radical media movements and positioning this collection of essays in relation to larger movements for social change.

In the media activist's toolbox are not only microphones and keyboards, but also markers, glue, film, spray-paint, and coloured pencils. Because the visual aspect of media activism is essential and full of imagination, the book contains unique art, graffiti, illustrations, and photography. Élise Gravel and Fanchon Esquieu illustrate autonomous media in all its forms and shapes with help of original *aquarelles* and *gouache* paintings. Within the following pages, the reader will also find photos of media activists in action by Québec City photographer Bernard Bastien, and photos of stencil-graffiti from around the world, provided by globe-trotting Dawn Paley. The work of these artists is interspersed with other stencil art and designs which caught the eye of Chester Rhoder, the book's graphic designer.

Like all documentation projects, this volume is not without its gaps and limitations. The come-and-go nature of autonomous media as well as their marginality and limited audiences has prevented the authors from using examples from every corner of this enormous country. Yet, an effort has been made to describe a wide range of practices developed in Canada and elsewhere.

It would have been suitable to detail such inspiring initiatives as the low power "radio barn-raisings" co-sponsored by the devoted people at the Prometheus Radio Project out of Philadelphia or to discuss music and DJ-ing as forms of autonomous media. Subversive and creative tactics, such as street theatre, puppet-making, and small press publishing, are also missing. We deliberately left out descriptions of innovative projects, such as *ÎleSansFil*, designed to promote free public wireless internet access in the Montréal area. Although this is part of recent developments that could serve the cause of guerrilla communications and prove useful for those who want to coordinate direct action from connected public spaces, we preferred to encourage analysis of autonomous media that already operate. The *ÎleSansFil* project, as well as other open source projects, catalyze new avenues of dissent that still need to be fully understood and exploited by media activists.

We have tried with insistence to enable the convergence of a wide variety of autonomous media creations to this project. If this objective has only been partially met, we believe that by taking a closer look at the many examples of autonomous media from the following chapters, the reader will encounter diversity.

There are some obvious omissions in this book project, such as the absence of media projects by and for Indigenous communities, illustrated amongst others by REDWIRE MAGAZINE, created by members of the Native Youth Movement, or the inspiring radio and television broadcasting in Nunavut and other Inuit territories. If there is to be a regret, it is definitely to have failed in amplifying voices of Indigenous writers and creators. Without wanting to excuse this particular blind spot, it is demonstrative of the general disconnect between Indigenous and non-Indigenous social and media activists. Although many activists bridge this unfortunate separation—such as demonstrated by NATIVE SOLIDARITY NEWS aired on CKUT radio in Montréal or the 2004 independent media centre set-up in Kanesatake, on Mohawk territory—most movements resisting corporate globalization in Canada do not specifically seek to voice indigenous discourse.

These blind spots were not intentional but definitely limit the dialogue we intended to make possible. Our aim was not to end-up with an all-encompassing encyclopaedia about what makes media subversive, but to trigger discussions and instill curiosity, encouraging readers to go out in search of more examples and to participate in the creation of media.

Many more books need to be written, and many more autonomous media projects need to be created, shared, and supported.

While we were both finishing our graduate work within the university, we had the desire to give back to the community. We wanted to share some of our observations and experiences as insiders of autonomous media projects along with those of the many activists and friends that work, most often voluntarily, to create autonomous structures and to disseminate alternative discourses. This collection of essays is the result of that first desire, the artefact that has grown out of the initial idea. We hope that this book inspires debate and discussions and that you, the reader, learn as much from it as we have from putting it together. In the spirit of autonomous media, we encourage readers to comment about elements of this book, whether you agree or disagree at: www.cumuluspress.com. We especially hope that perusing the words and illustrations within its pages, you will be inspired to activate resistance and dissent.

notes

[1] Cadorette, Patrick. (October 2004). Montréal. Personal interview. Cadorette is a member of Québec Indymedia and volunteers at Radio Centre-Ville, a community radio station, both in Montréal.

[2] The ideas presented here on social movements, media, and access to meaning-making were originally developed in Andrea Langlois' Master's thesis. Langlois, Andrea. (2004). *Mediating Transgressions: The Global Justice Movement and Canadian News Media.* Unpublished Master's Thesis. Concordia University. Available online at: http://ase.ath.cx/hosted/liberterre/memoire.pdf.

[3] For more on the history of self-publishing in Canadian anarchist communities, see: Allan Antliff (ed.). (2004). *Only A Beginning: An Anarchist Anthology.* Vancouver: Arsenal Pulp Press.

[4] Michel Sénécal develops these logics and explains their interplay in Sénécal, Michel. (1995). *L'espace médiatique. Les communications à l'épreuve de la démocratie.* Montréal: Liber.

web resources

Centre for Aboriginal Media: www.imaginenative.org
ÎleSansFil: www.ilesansfil.org
Native Solidarity News: www.ckut.ca/nsn
Pink Panthers: www.lespantheresroses.org
Prometheus Radio Project: www.prometheusradio.org
Redwire Magazine: www.redwiremag.com

media activists and social movements

by scott uzelman

HARD
AT WORK IN

Running bamboo often gives rise to unwitting bamboo gardeners. A single innocent shoot can stand alone for several years and then suddenly an entire field of bamboo begins to sprout. This leaves the unsuspecting gardener with a new bamboo garden that stubbornly resists attempts to get rid of it. While on the surface each shoot appears to be an individual, related but separate from its neighbours, underground all are connected through a complex network of root-like stems and filaments called a rhizome.[1] During the years the gardener watched a single bamboo shoot grow tall, underground the bamboo rhizome grew horizontally, spreading throughout the yard, storing nutrients in anticipation of a coming spring. Like the bamboo garden, social movements are often rhizomatic organisms growing horizontally into new terrains, establishing connections just below the surface of everyday life, eventually bursting forth in unpredictable ways. And there, unseen amongst the grassroots, facilitating rhizomatic growth, work the media activists.

Media activists are crucial catalysts in movements for social and environmental justice. This chapter begins with a brief exploration of social movements as localized and networked communities of resistance that are dependent upon communication for their continued existence and growth. It then turns to the people who take up communication-centred struggles and examines their tactics and strategies. A distinction is made between alternative media activists, those who work to reform mainstream media, and autonomous media activists, those who seek to bypass mainstream media by fostering new forms of participatory and democratic communication. By directly confronting the mainstream corporate media, or by taking direct action to bypass them altogether, media activists facilitate the spread of social movement rhizomes.

imagined communities of resistance and struggle

We often speak of social movements as if they are creatures with a coherent will of their own, as entities we can see and point to. But in reality there are no such objects to observe. Even the massive demonstrations against the institutions of corporate rule—the International Monetary Fund, World Bank, World Trade Organization, or imperialist oil wars in the Middle East—are not in themselves social movements. Just as the single bamboo stalk is only a localized extension of a larger organism, demonstrations, uprisings, revolts, and even

revolutions are only the manifestation of social forces that are larger, more resilient and more widespread than these outbursts of popular discontent. "Social movement," then, is just the shorthand we use to refer to the often diffuse and fluid communities of individuals and groups who resist various oppressive forms of power and control. Perhaps more importantly, social movements work to create democratic alternatives and to improve the conditions in which we live. These communities are, as Benedict Anderson famously stated,[2] largely imagined in that while most activists generally circulate within a dense network of fellow dissidents, they will never meet all of them in their local area, let alone the millions of people world-wide who are involved in similar struggles.

Communities of struggle and transformation are thus communicative phenomena. Social movements are dependent upon the establishment and maintenance of local spaces and diffuse networks of communication through which communities are imagined, developed, and mobilized for action.

Communication within social movements often grows like the bamboo rhizome—horizontally, in multiple directions, from many points, without a centre or clear hierarchy. These flows of communication are often experimental and unplanned; social movements frequently adopt new modes of communication and adapt them to meet their needs. Various communication technologies allow dispersed people and groups to foster a sense of connectedness, to recognize common interests and causes as they share their critiques of inequality and unaccountable power, their successes, defeats, strategies, future plans, and so on. Yet, despite the proliferation and global reach of communication technologies, creating such spaces is not an easy task. Social movements often confront near monopolies over the means of communication in the form of corporate media conglomerates and even public broadcasting systems. So much, then, depends upon the media activists.

mainstream media and the mushroom treatment

"The media," my dad never tires of saying, "subject us to the mushroom treatment. They keep us in the dark and feed us lots of shit." On this he wouldn't get much disagreement from people involved in social movements. Many excellent books have been devoted to the problem of the corporate media which cannot be summed up in this short chapter.[3] What must be

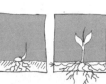

emphasized here are the ways in which the corporate media function to undermine the growth and development of resisting communities.

At the risk of drastically over-simplifying the problem, there are two primary impediments to any project that seeks to manufacture dissent. First, while social movements are dependent upon the circulation of what we might call counter-information—information critical of the status quo—the very structure, institutional interests, and routines of mainstream, corporate media effectively act as blockades to dissenting opinion. Giant, horizontally and vertically integrated media corporations have little reason to give sustained coverage to voices critical of the conditions in which such entities thrive. This is not to say that the media are completely blind to the excesses of capitalism, abuses of power by the powerful, routine acts of injustice perpetrated by dominant institutions, and so on. We are all too often exposed to images of horrific oil and chemical spills, sordid tales of corporate fraud and political scandal, for example. However, these sad stories are often individualized, lacking in history and context, and abbreviated into easily digestible sound bite explanations—a drunken oil tanker captain here, a few bad apples there.

On systemic issues, the media are, not surprisingly, almost asleep. For example, media corporations have no interest in challenging the spread of neoliberal economic dogma in any serious way because they benefit from decreased regulation, reduced corporate taxation, weakened organized labour, and so on. Indeed, in this race to the bottom they have been more like cheerleaders than watchdogs. On the growth of corporate power and simultaneous erosion of democratic processes and institutions, the media have little to say. They also have no interest in presenting a sustained challenge to the environmental damage wrought by consumer capitalism given their commercial function in attracting audiences to sell to advertisers. Name an oppressive form of power—patriarchy, racism, colonialism, ageism, homophobia, etc.—and it doesn't take much looking to find an example where the media has opted to exploit the negative representations that prop it up. In other words, on the issues around which social movements often congeal, the media tend to look the other way at best and, at worst, deliberately or unintentionally support them.

These tendencies are only reinforced by the mainstream media's privileging unidirectional communicative relationships. As mass media— commercial

television, radio, newspapers, and, to a lesser extent, the internet—privilege a one-way flow of information and entertainment, offer very few opportunities for public participation in the creation of content.[4] This is not just a product of technological form but rather of the manner in which media institutions have been constructed historically as profit-seeking, private businesses. The public tends to be positioned as consumers and only rarely as producers of content; people are encouraged to see themselves as spectators rather than participants.

This brings us to a second general point. The profitability of the corporate media depends on their ability to cultivate a specific type of person. In order to keep their customers happy (i.e., advertisers), the corporate media actively encourage us to see ourselves as individual, self-interested, acquisitive consumers rather than as collective, community-minded, inquisitive citizens. As vectors of advertising, the world they present tends to be de-politicized, a-historical, somewhat random, inevitable, and eternal. Any problems we might face are a product of our own individual failures and are solvable primarily through hard work (i.e., paid employment) and product purchases. In this land of market-believe, the good life becomes a lifetime of shopping, where freedom equals wealth, and solidarity means supporting the local pro-hockey team.

From these few points of a much larger critique of the mainstream, corporate media, it is clear that they represent an imposing barrier to movements for social and environmental justice.

hard at work amongst the rhizomes

The sorry state of the media system in most countries has inspired people the world over to challenge dominant media institutions, whether they are corporate or state-run, and to begin the work of building their own democratic media. A diverse range of activists and groups have employed numerous strategies to put an end to the mushroom treatment. Media activists have worked to: a) open the mainstream media to a wider range of ideas and perspectives; b) subvert dominant cultural, commercial, and political messages; c) reform media practices and ownership structures through regulatory or legal pressure; and/or d) bypass the dominant media system by creating forms of participatory and democratic communication that often radically break with established traditions. We might even see these world-wide efforts to challenge mainstream media as a unique social movement—a media democracy movement.

This is not to say that there is some imagined community of pure media activists that is distinct and separate from other social movements. Rather, media activists, and media activist collectives and organizations generally work within the more encompassing contemporary movement of movements to which we append various adjectives—anti-corporate globalization, pro-democracy, anti-capitalist, global justice, etc. Broadly speaking, we might call anyone who works to challenge or bypass the mainstream media a media activist. This broad definition would probably capture all sorts of people who focus their energies on the problem of the mainstream media. It also includes those who don't consider themselves media activists but who recognize that their concerns will be ignored or marginalized by the corporate media unless action is taken against them. But again, we shouldn't fall into the trap of thinking about pure media activists versus dabblers. Even activists who have made media democracy their primary focus also tend to involve themselves in other movements (e.g. environmental, women's, anti-racist, labour, etc.).

Media activists don't fit a typical age, gender, race, or class profile. They are found in so-called developing countries and in over-developed countries. They come from the ranks of the poor and from the affluent, the young and the old. Some practice their media activism in their spare time away from work and others are full-time, paid or unpaid, activists. They are sometimes professional lobbyists, lawyers, unionists, or workers in non-profit organizations. Some are students, others are teachers or academics. They can be musicians, artists, writers, photographers and videographers; a lot of them are Jacks or Jills of many trades. What motivates people from all walks of life to struggle to change the mediascape in which we live stems from a general recognition that the tools of communication that play such a central role in our lives are put to use in very limited ways, for very narrow purposes, and for the benefit of a small minority of wealthy

"freedom to love and feel"

individuals. It is a struggle that often takes place beyond the eye of the mainstream media (for obvious reasons), tucked away amongst the grassroots.

strategies of media activists: alternatives vs. autonomy

With this broad definition and sketch of the media activist in mind, it is helpful to make a distinction between two general strategies employed to remedy the problem of the mainstream, corporate media. Within the media democratization movement we can see a split between alternative media strategies and autonomous media strategies.[5] Whereas the former focus primarily on changing mainstream media content, the latter seek also to change the ways we communicate by encouraging participation and dialogue.

Alternative media strategies are those that focus primarily on challenging the mainstream media to become more accountable to the publics they claim to serve, or on using existing media structures and processes to distribute counter-information. Media activists committed to this strategy have employed a colourful collage of tactics. For example, a number of organizations have attempted to challenge corporate control through legislative or legal processes, in particular around ownership rules (e.g., the Campaign for Press and Broadcasting Freedom in the U.K. or the Council of Canadians in Canada). Others have sought to defend and expand public broadcasting; in Canada, Friends of Canadian Broadcasting has been on the frontlines against the continued onslaught against the CBC by right-wing pundits and political parties. Some campaigns have been carried out by media workers themselves to preserve their autonomy from the commercial logic of employers. Many groups, Greenpeace being the most famous, have become masters at opening spaces for dissent by manipulating media coverage through the production of spectacular events. We can also think of campaigns to better educate media consumers on the blind spots, double standards, biases, and effects of corporate media, through media literacy (e.g., Check Your Head or Media Education Foundation) and media analysis and monitoring (e.g., NewsWatch Canada, Fairness and Accuracy in Reporting [FAIR] or Project Censored) as alternative media strategies.

At the heart of this strategy, whatever form it takes, is a concern with disseminating counter or alternative information. What remains largely unchallenged, however, is one of the key logics guiding the mass media—the privileging of one-way flows of information from the media to consumers. In other words, content and not form tends to be the central issue for alternative media activists.

Autonomous media strategies, on the other hand, attempt to bypass the mainstream media through experimentation with new forms of democratic communication that are relatively independent from corporate and government power.[6] Not only do autonomous media function as channels through which dissident perspectives can flow but they also often seek to foster new, more democratic and participatory ways of communicating. Where the hierarchical, point-to-mass structure of the mainstream media privileges representation and monologue, autonomous media often are much more open to democratic decision-making, popular participation in the creation of content, and dialogue between participants. In fact, many of them require it.

Autonomous media strategies often involve establishing more democratic and participatory forms of television, radio, print, and internet-based media. For people committed to autonomous media, it is not enough to open the mainstream media to a wider range of voices. We must also radically democratize the means of communication. To do so, autonomous media activists take up the tools of communication in order to tell their own stories. For instance, as prices have fallen, the video camera has become increasingly popular with autonomous media activists. We see video cameras employed at protests the world over to provide coverage of the events and issues at stake. The images produced by these individuals or collectives then often appear on community access television (e.g., Paper Tiger Television) as streaming video through websites (e.g., Guerrilla News Network), or in documentaries (e.g., Big Noise Films). However, autonomous media producers don't limit themselves to expensive technology; autonomous print projects (e.g. newspapers, handbills, and pamphlets) thrive in neighbourhoods around the world. Regardless of the tools they take up, autonomous media activists are distinguished by their commitment to an egalitarian, do-it-yourself, anti-authoritarian ethic in the struggle for democratic media.

Autonomous media activists also encourage and help others

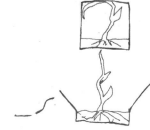

to produce their own media products. They often do so by sharing skills through workshops and hands-on training sessions in which people are taught to use, for example, digital video and audio equipment, computer-based editing equipment, or are given tips for writing good eyewitness or investigative reports. This practice is carried out by Undercurrents, a group of video activists in Wales that is committed to encouraging and training people to use video for covering and disseminating issues and events routinely ignored by the mainstream media. In a less direct way, autonomous media activists are also teachers by way of the good examples they provide. Their very existence demonstrates what people with a few resources and a lot of boldness, energy, creativity, and commitment can do to become the media and democratize the means and processes of communication.

Autonomous media strategies also include experiments with new communication technologies. Here we can think of email as a powerful tool of dialogue and information dissemination, one that helped to defeat the initial negotiations for the Multilateral Agreement on Investment.[7] Cell phones and text messaging are also becoming increasingly useful in activating and coordinating spontaneous uprisings, notably in Venezuela (see below) and in the Philippines during the popular uprising, People Power II, in 2001, against the Estrada government.[8] Those autonomous media activists with technical skills like computer programming, webpage design, or electronic hardware maintenance play crucial roles in these sorts of experiments. A great deal of the energy and new ideas behind the Independent Media Centre movement, for instance, were generated by these skilled individuals as they worked to design and enhance the software behind the websites, to maintain the computer servers, to train others in these skills, and so on.

Besides experimenting with new communication technologies, autonomous media activists often engage in various forms of critique through artistic expression such as culture jamming or adbusting, billboard liberation, political graffiti and murals, street theatre and other forms of performance art, such as DJ-ing. To the extent that these forms of expression encourage public participation in the act of criticism, they are moving beyond the consumptive relationship encouraged by mass media. With this in mind, we could also include pamphlet or leaflet distribution, stickering, or postering in a list of autonomous media tactics.

Of course, alternative and autonomous media strategies are not mutually exclusive; many media activists and groups employ both strategies as needed. Independent Community Television (ICTV) in Vancouver, a small cooperative of grassroots video producers that encourages public access to community TV, serves as a good example of the fusing of both strategies. In 2001, ICTV applied to the Canadian Radio-Television and Telecommunications Commission, the federal regulator of broadcasting in Canada, for a low-power broadcasting license in order to operate a non-profit television station that would serve Vancouver communities. Although their request had not yet been granted as of the writing of this essay, ICTV stands as a good example of an autonomous media collective that has attempted to use government regulation to open up spaces for autonomous media within the existing mediascape.

Regardless of how we classify these experiments, what is important to keep in mind are the logics that guide different facets of media activism. The different logics are important not only to the way we conduct our politics but also to the way we conceive social change. Alternative media strategies, by demanding change of powerful institutions, in some respects take for granted the legitimacy of these powerful institutions. They may ask for more balanced news reporting or limits to violent entertainment. However, they don't demand that media corporations stop promoting endless consumption through advertising and they rarely advocate for public access to corporate media-making facilities. Rather, alternative media activists demand that the mainstream media temper undesirable behaviours and make room for other perspectives within existing formats. Autonomous media strategies, on the other hand, do not "clothe the emperor" by appealing to dominant institutions for justice. Instead, they work to undermine and subvert them through direct action to fulfill local needs in the here and now.

helping the bamboo garden to blossom

The sceptic might look at autonomous media practices as little more than interesting but marginal experiments with little effect, something akin to pissing one's self in a dark blue suit: you get instant relief, you feel warm all over for awhile, and pretty much no one notices. If we take a narrow view and point at the small activist newspaper, or the local micro-radio station on their own, then the blue suit metaphor might ring true, especially to those who count success in terms of audience size alone.

However, looking at individual autonomous media examples is a bit like looking at a single filament of a larger rhizome. By taking the part to represent the whole, we fail to recognize each autonomous media experiment's interconnectedness with a much larger organism. When we look at autonomous media as a whole—as a complex media mesh of experiments in democratic communication—the number of people noticing increases exponentially.

Two recent examples stand out. First, we can think of the success of the Independent Media Centre (IMC) movement which, especially during large-scale events such as the 2001 Free Trade Area of the Americas (FTAA) in Québec City or the 2004 demonstrations against the Republican National Convention in New York, has routinely drawn hundreds of thousands, if not millions, of people to its network of websites. Not only was the IMC network a focal point for people interested in the issues and events surrounding these protests, but it also served as a way for information to be distributed to other autonomous media projects.

A second example can be seen in a more localized event, one that had an impact on an entire region. During the coup against Venezuelan president Hugo Chavez in 2002, grassroots media played a key role in thwarting the attempt to overthrow the elected government. Because the mainstream media celebrated the coup and refused to cover the initial demonstrations in the streets, and resistance by elements of the military, community media proved invaluable in bypassing corporate control of the means of mass communication. Grassroots radio and television stations broadcasted the initial resistance to the coup and consequently helped to mobilize tens of thousands of people who took to the streets in protest. The resistance was further amplified through the use of cell phones to distribute information and mobilize popular resistance. Two days after it had begun, thanks in part to grassroots media, the coup regime collapsed.[9]

We may advocate for autonomous media practice for the simple reason that it seems unlikely that governments—the majority of which seem to be under the sway of free market ideology—will move to regulate the mainstream media or to spend the money necessary for public broadcasters to fulfill their public service mandate. And asking for media corporations to willingly change is a bit like asking a tiger to become vegetarian. Faced with these obstacles, the way towards media democratization may not only be through the mainstream media but may also require going around them. Rather than waiting for the powerful to be swayed by the force of our arguments, it might prove more effective to get on with the work of experimenting with autonomous media in the hope that we can help the rhizomes of social movements to flourish so that one day they might rise up from below and blossom into beautiful new bamboo gardens and a full-fledged media democracy movement.

notes

[1] The rhizome metaphor comes from Deleuze, Gilles & Felix Guattari. (1987). *A Thousand Plateaus: Capitalism and Schizophrenia.* London, U.K.: Athlone Press. They use the metaphor to describe horizontally linked, non-hierarchical forms of social organization, thought, communication, etc. (pgs. 3-25).

[2] For information about the notion of imagined communities, please see: Anderson, Benedict. (1991). *Imagined Communities: Reflections on the Origin and Spread of Nationalism.* Revised Edition. London, U.K. & New York: Verso.

[3] More complete critiques of the corporate media include: Nichols, John & Robert W. McChesney. (2000). *It's the Media, Stupid.* New York: Seven Stories Press; Shoemaker, Pamela J. & Stephen D. Reese (1996). *Mediating the Message: Theories of Influences On Mass Media Content.* 2nd Edition. New York: Longman; Hackett, Robert A. & Gruneau, Richard. (2000). *The Missing News: Filters and Blind Spots in Canada's Press.* Ottawa: Canadian Centre for Policy Alternatives; and Herman, Edward & Noam Chomsky. (1988). *Manufacturing Consent: The Political Economy of the Mass Media.* New York: Pantheon Books. For a recent empirical study of the influence of corporate power on the media, see Hackett, Robert A. and Scott Uzelman. (2003). "Tracing Corporate Influences on Press Content: A Summary of Recent NewsWatch Canada Research," *Journalism Studies.* Vol. 4 (3): pgs. 331-346.

[4] Of course, the internet offers unprecedented opportunities for dialogue through email and information dissemination through web pages. However, corporations still hold the balance of power in attracting audiences to commercially-oriented websites through advertising and in their ability to guide the development of the internet.

[5] The distinction I make between autonomous and alternative media strategies originally appeared in a Master's thesis I completed at Simon Fraser University. See Uzelman, Scott. (2002). *Catalyzing Participatory Communication: Independent Media Centre and the Politics of Direct Action.* Unpublished Master's thesis: Simon Fraser University. Published online at: http://www.global.indymedia.org.au/local/webcast/uploads/thesis-complete_pdf_.pdf [accessed July 12, 2004].

[6] For readers interested in more examples of autonomous media projects, portal-type webpages are always a good place to start. For a list of autonomous radio stations throughout North America visit Alternative Radio's website. Media Channel provides an extensive database of autonomous media organizations and media activist resources. Free Speech TV is a useful starting point for finding autonomous TV and video projects.

[7] The Multilateral Agreement on Investment (MAI) was a sweeping trade agreement that would have greatly reduced the ability of governments to regulate corporate direct investment. The negotiations, carried out in secrecy by the Organization for Economic Co-operation and Development, stalled in 1998, in part because of grassroots resistance organized largely via email and the internet. However, despite the initial victory, the idea of the MAI seems to live on in smaller regional agreements that continue to be negotiated. For more information on the MAI see: Clarke, Tony & Maude Barlow. (1997). *MAI: The Multilateral Agreement on Investment and the Threat to Canadian Sovereignty*. Toronto: Stoddart. For more information on the grassroots resistance to the MAI, see: Dyer-Witheford, Nick. (1999). *Cyber-Marx: Cycles and Circuits of Struggle in High-Technology Capitalism*. Urbana and Chicago: University of Illinois Press, pgs. 229-230.

[8] For readers interested in the use of cell phones during the People Power II uprising, see: Rafael, Vicente. (2003). "The Cell Phone and the Crowd: Messianic Politics in the Contemporary Philippines," *Public Culture*. Vol. 15 (3), pgs. 399-425.

[9] For more information on the role of the corporate media in the attempted coup in Venezuela, see: Everton, Robert. (forthcoming 2005). "Media, Civil Society and the Dynamics of Regime Change in Venezuela." *Global Communications: Towards a Transcultural Political Economy*, Paula Chakravartty et al. (eds). Durham: Duke University Press. For discussion of the role of alternative media in grassroots resistance to the coup, see: Wilpert, Gregory. (2003). *Community Media in Venezuela*. Published online at: http://www.venezuelanalysis.com/articles.php?artno=1054. [accessed August 23, 2004].

"not one more death, not one woman less"

Ni una Muerte + ni una Mujer menos

Memoria Feminista

"every day, i wash my brain with tv"

web resources

Adbusters: www.adbusters.org
Alternative Radio: www.alternativeradio.org
Big Noise Films: www.bignoisefilms.com
Campaign for Press and Broadcasting Freedom (Canada): www.presscampaign.org
Campaign for Press and Broadcasting Freedom (UK): www.cpbf.org.uk
Check Your Head: www.checkyourhead.org
Council of Canadians: www.canadians.org
Fairness and Accuracy in Reporting (FAIR): www.fair.org
Free Speech TV: www.freespeech.org
Friends of Canadian Broadcasting: www.friends.ca
Guerrilla News Network: www.guerrillanews.com
Independent Community Television: www.vcn.bc.ca/ictv/1pages/welcome.htm
Independent Media Centre: www.indymedia.org
Media Channel: www.mediachannel.org
Media Education Foundation: www.mediaed.org
NewsWatch Canada: www.sfu.ca/cmns/research/newswatch/intro.html
Paper Tiger Television: www.papertiger.org
Project Censored: www.projectcensored.org
Undercurrents: www.undercurrents.org

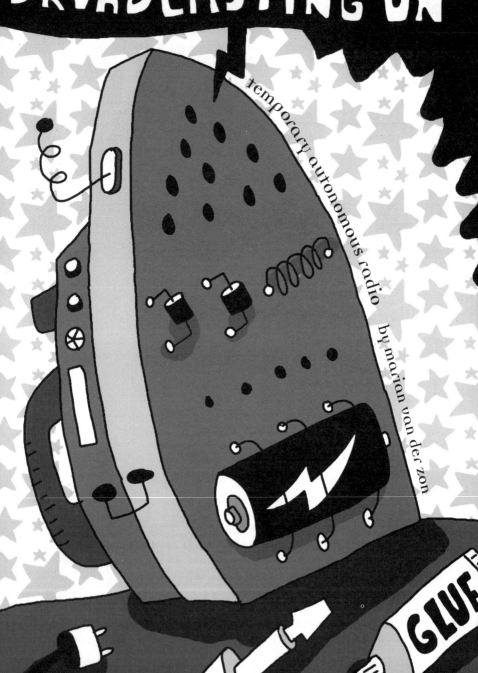

OUR OWN TERMS

Welcome. You are listening to TAR, Temporary Autonomous Radio. Today we'll be speaking about the history and philosophy of TAR. TAR is relatively new to the airwaves and today can be found at 90.7 FM here in sunny Montréal.

And so, TAR is a one-watt FM band Micro-radio station. I built TAR as an alternative and autonomous source of media. It was certainly inspired by Hakim Bey, an anarchist particularly known for his work around Temporary Autonomous Zones, which he conceptualized as islands or hideouts from our capitalist, consumer-based society, pirate-based intentional communities, if you will.[1] Groups of individuals would rise up and create information networks that were temporary and geographically flexible. Like Temporary Autonomous Zones, TAR strives to be a recurring

> "Micro-radio lets us speak for ourselves, lets us keep our radios on and take down those fiddles from the wall. By blurring the boundaries between mass media and face-to-face interaction, it puts the former at the disposal of the latter."[2] — Jesse Walker

a historical foray into radio

Radio was originally derived from military research and development, with a focus on using radio communication to facilitate social control by the state. It is therefore promising and ironic that there have been increasing avenues for revolutionary involvement in a genre of media with these origins. Radio was initially conceived to benefit the interests of the political, military, and economic powers. According to Robert W. McChesney,[3] professor of communications and the author of eight books on media and politics, in the first half of the 1920s, radio began to be accessible to the public and several hundred non-profit broadcasters (the majority were

illegal pirate action that is both temporary and moveable, with alternative content motivated by the participants... and yes, this means you. As such, TAR strives to be radical in terms of its broadcasting philosophy and in terms of its content from contributors. As well, one of the mandates of TAR is to spread the word and encourage others to build their own radio stations—to plug into a network of radical culture.

Radio is easy. Radio is accessible. Start where you will. Come on in and share your world with our listeners. Or build your own world. I can assure you that I too was as novice as they come. But with a willingness to learn, a little experimentation, a community of voices willing to

affiliated to universities and colleges) emerged as the real pioneers of U.S. broadcasting. They were overtaken by corporate, profit-minded interests by the end of the 1920s, a trend that has only increased in the years since.

Criticisms and thus awareness around radio's inaccessibility increased in the 1930s. German poet and playwright, Bertolt Brecht[4]—a well-known name in radio—wanted radio to be a multi-way system of communication. Radio was used in a one-sided manner. This meant that while there were many ears listening only a few mouths were speaking. Brecht realized that the democratic aspect of radio was lost in this model. He was interested in the interactive nature of radio and felt that the audience should be both broadcaster and listener. In other words, every listener should be able to speak as well as to hear.

Access to the airwaves is as important today as it was then. While not every listener wants to be actively engaged with radio, the challenge is to

takeover the airwaves, and imagination, your very own radio station can be born.

come in to the world of activist radio

Why am I here? I love radio... micro-radio, pirate radio, community radio, public radio, corporate radio... local, national, international... some would argue that so long as it is radio, it is a good start. Who's kidding who? Some radio is obviously better than others.

I have held a lifelong passion for radio. Music lovers speak about the sound of the turntable needle hitting vinyl as food for the soul. For me, the component of radio that has always spoken the loudest is the innate capacity within it for imagination. Like other forms of media, there are

create and provide space for those who do want to speak and be heard. At present, the ownership of radio, like other forms of media, lies increasingly in the hands of a few. The monopolizing of public airwaves for private interest opinions and contributions has led to increasingly homogenized content. The result is a corporate radio format with shallow coverage of politics and limited diversity in the views presented. Access must include room for all interested parties to become involved, in terms of content, context, and technology.

Activist individuals and groups have, increasingly, taken it upon themselves to engage with radio and, consequently, the ways in which we can access the airwaves continue to expand, from micro to macro approaches. As the number of avenues for access increases, the possibilities for shared resources and collaboration between practitioners of micro-radio, pirate radio, community radio, and internet streaming gain strength.

Resources can be shared in a number of ways. For example, micro-radio becomes pirate radio when its transmission range extends beyond the national legal limits. These limits vary from country to country, but as a general rule, any broadcast over five watts

many ways imagination can be incorporated into radio—technically, contextually—through content, and above all, in the ways it is received and engaged with by you, the listener. The capacity to imagine within radio is music to my ears.

The capacity to imagine holds within it the ability to be discerning. It holds with it the ability to be alternatively-minded, autonomously-minded, radical, and revolutionary.

Alternatively-minded folks tend to approach radio from the perspective of content. An autonomous approach seeks to address not only content, but also the structure of radio, allowing room for non-hierarchical self-organized

is deemed to be a pirate broadcast and consequently, a criminal act. A low cost micro-radio station can be built for a mere 20 dollars, while internet streaming start-up costs begin at 1000 dollars. Increasingly, micro- and pirate radio practitioners with little financial backing are invited by larger organizations to use internet streaming already in place. This piggy-backing can provide room for safer involvement in situations where micro- and pirate radio are repressed by a government that actively criminalizes micro-broadcasters. Micro- and pirate radio practitioners can upload their audio onto the internet in a clandestine manner. By sharing these resources, activists are able to build global networks, offering an alternative vision of our world, and challenging the corporate control over media at a fraction of the cost.

Following Hakim Bey's concept of the Temporary Autonomous Zone, activists have striven to make pirate radio, micro-radio, and community radio into autonomous and often temporary experiments. Examples are plenty. Pirate Radio Caroline appeared in the guise of a pirate ship off the coast of Great Britain for the first time in 1964 to offer up the rebellious music of the time and it still broadcasts today. It was soon followed by a number of vessels, quickly latching onto loopholes in British law that allowed more personal freedom of content and control over Britain's airwaves when broadcasting from international waters. Pirate radio has flourished since then and has continued to do so with a diversity of content and intent across the globe.

goal is to take over the airwaves, whether concerning production and maintenance of a radio station, the community experience, the dissemination of marginalized content, or all three combined.

And right now, taking over the airwaves, you are listening to TAR, Temporary Autonomous Radio at 90.7 FM in Montréal. TAR has broadcast from a number of locations in Montréal, Toronto, and Victoria, and today we are talking about TAR's philosophy and creation. We have been talking about the revolutionary possibilities of radio. TAR addresses all three aspects of radio: technology, context, and content.

Micro-radio has also prospered, on a smaller-scale. Some micro-radio operators have chosen to organize themselves by linking up in a series that expanded their transmission/reception range significantly. Other operators are interested in affecting a smaller geographical area for more specialized programming. Community radio tends to be more traditional in technological structure, and like micro- and pirate radio, can be notable for broadcasting alternative- or subculture-specific news, music, and commentary. It often strives to include voices that are typically marginalized. Its members also are more inclined to organize non-hierarchically.

And with possibilities come limitations. Some of the criticisms of community radio include accusations that it is too closely linked with university institutions, that it is not accessible enough, or that it is too accessible at the expense of quality. Involvement on an organizational level is possible, and yet often limited by chair boards and tight social networks. Furthermore, within Canada the CRTC only allows a limited number of licenses and the range of each station varies.

When we turn the gaze to micro-radio, it is criticized for being low-tech, for being ineffective due to its limited range, and for broadcasting what some would consider questionable material, which might include casual

LET ME SPEAK TO YOU ABOUT CONTENT

The broadcast content of TAR is varied to say the least. We strive for a theme of alternative content, which includes spoken word, music, radio art, and radio karaoke. The spoken word tends towards varied social justice issues, not only those related to making radio. Our music leans in the direction of the seldom heard. Our radio art is varied and our very own radio karaoke is another attempt to foster community involvement. Radio karaoke completes every broadcast session, including today's, and consists of rousing renditions of well-known songs. While those in the studio do their karaoke thing, singing in the microphone along with their chosen tune, the listener is encouraged to

conversation, bodily sound effects, or amateur musicianship. Pirate radio is also disparaged for a perceived lack of audience and, of course, while the illegal nature is appealing to some, it is a serious limitation to others.

the importance of content

For many activist radio broadcasters, alternative content is a given. For some, what is broadcast is more important then the technology itself. For this reason, some media activists choose to work inside the corporate media, striving to provide alternative information to a larger audience. This could include extending news coverage to include issues that are relevant to particular ethnic groups, for example. They are interested in swaying larger public opinion within the limits of the corporate format.

At the other end of the spectrum, autonomous radio is criticized for a lack of audience and is therefore deemed ineffective. Alternately, there is the argument that the people involved are preaching to the converted. Perhaps so. Yet, it is important to recognize that autonomous radio can have different purposes. According to Gretchen King,[5] a long time radio activist, micro- or pirate radio can be used to disseminate tactical information or it can be a space within which to develop and share analysis around specific issues. Examples of tactical information could be in the context of a street mobilization, where the movements of police are broadcast, the movement of protesters is suggested, or simply to broadcast the locations

participatory way. Regardless of its success, the impetus behind it is to provide a community feel and a new form of radio experience.

Everyone is welcome to be part of the content of TAR. You are welcome to come into the studio. Wander down Fabre Street, look for the TAR banner draped over our balcony, wander on up, and say hello. We are set-up very casually and have had a lot of first-timers on the air. I remember the first broadcast. It was wonderful. I had a friend stop by with his family: his mother, his aunt, his grandmother. These three generations gathered around the microphone to tell generational family stories and embarrass the youngest. These are people who would never usually get the

of food and other amenities. Additionally, micro- and pirate radio can be used to generate collective memory and encourage historical reflection, especially if broadcasts are archived.

In either instance, micro- and pirate radio work to build community and therefore promote direct engagement. They allow practitioners to post opinions and information via the internet, through streaming, or directly onto the FM dial. As a consequence, this brings Temporary Autonomous Zones, like street mobilizations, to the larger public. From city to city, there is often a common area on the FM band where radio pirates tend to congregate and listeners make it a habit of tuning in to listen. In Montréal this frequency varies from around 90.3, 101, and 104 on the FM dial and in Vancouver, 89.3 FM is a favourite.

contextual considerations for democratic radio

While individuals working within corporate-owned media structures are limited to dealing with content, autonomous radio practitioners can go one step further, concentrating on how radio is organized and what this tangibly means for those involved in the radio project.

to speak their lives out over the airwaves. For all of you who have yet to engage... come on up to TAR: speak your minds!

AND THEN THERE ARE THE CONTEXTUAL CONSIDERATIONS

TAR was built to encourage active community involvement. Given TAR's three block range, every time we broadcast, a small listening community is assumed. Perhaps you have seen the posters in your neighbourhood. Because of our limited range, as I have already mentioned, TAR provides an accessible radio experience that is not intimidating to first-time broadcasters. And yet, we can still create a viable and alternative information-sharing pool for a select communi-

Democratic radio is increasingly a priority for those with an activist bent. In his article "Organizing Democratic Radio," John L. Hochheimer[6] argues that democratic radio requires three aspects: the extension of democracy, acknowledgement and encouragement of a pluralist society through media (radio), and centralized decision-making within the institution/station. Radio organizations like Radio Free Cascadia—an online centre for free radio activism coming out of the Cascadia region of Oregon—strive to understand the connections and structures of power in order to proceed with the organization of a truly democratic station. They do this by developing non-hierarchical systems of organization by using committees, free distribution of information and resources. Radio Free Cascadia also uses an online organizing centre to promote local and long-distance participation in its activities. It is this autonomous approach that defines Radio Free Cascadia and which guarantees alternative content.

Micro-radio works to link people together. Radio becomes a space (both the studio and the airwaves) where the line between those who make radio and those who consume radio is blurred. Diverse ideas, cultures, experiences, and politics are shared within the group producing radio as well as with the audiences in front of their radios. Because micro-radio usually has a weak signal, the purpose changes from broadcasting to narrowcasting. Aside from those listening, it inspires inexperienced individuals to get involved and promotes a sense of community or action.

ly. All of our broadcasts occur close to a village within the city and word spreads quickly.

Start talking. Come on in; tell your friends. The more contributors we have, the more often we can take over the airwaves. When TAR contributors and supporters gather in TAR's common room to prepare, relax, and listen, the radio experience for the broadcaster/contributor/listener is encompassing. When TAR becomes background noise due to conversation, the intent to dialogue is present and a community is coalescing. With time, this tight community can grow around any Micro-radio station. TAR seeks to encourage community involvement and share knowledge around social issues, culture jamming, alternative media, obscure

Tetsuo Kogawa[7] experienced this phenomenon first-hand in Japan through the 1980s and came to believe that the potential for mini-FM lies in the communication opportunities for the individuals involved rather than in the purpose of broadcasting. Regardless of how many people are listening, he saw that there is an inherent value in re-organizing groups of people and communities into producers of media. Isolated people could find company, speak thoughts, and share ideas in a locale where dialogue is encouraged. This is impossible in a commercial situation where the bottom line needs to show profit. Micro-radio works particularly well in densely populated areas, such as Tokyo, because a one-watt FM micro-radio broadcasting a half-mile radius can potentially access 10,000 listeners, if they manage to find a less-used frequency on the band.

The potential for autonomous radio is a major draw for anyone who is interested in an organizational structure that is anti-authoritarian and consensus-based. It is this organizational structure that allows for a deeper understanding of the hierarchical structures of power that have come to dominate mainstream media and the information we receive. The type of radio produced by a community news collective, for example, exposes the biases of mainstream news. News produced from the grassroots, within the community, privileges the experiences of the marginalized and will generally focus on stories that avoid reinforcing the status quo. Those living within a community thus become experts on their social real-

spontaneous, creative participation. Come on up, loosen your tongues, use our resources to begin your own station. Revolutionize your life.

WHAT ABOUT EQUIPMENT AND TECHNOLOGY? WHERE DO I START?

When I decided to build TAR I was a newbie. I knew nothing of circuit boards, oscillators, transistors, capacitors, resistors. What was a girl to do? I picked brains, surfed the net, ordered a 20-dollar kit online, and soon was experimenting with soldering. In short you just need to look, listen, and learn. You might undergo an immense learning curve.

ity, something that is rarely seen within mainstream news, which privileges the voices of big business, government officials, and academic experts.

embracing the possibilities of technology

Because radio technology is relatively cheap, opportunities for activists to start their own revolutionary radio projects abound. Or, for those already engaged, to push the limits by becoming more experienced and inclusive. For some, this might simply take the form of using a more powerful transmitter and moving from the world of micro- to pirate radio. For others, projects could include using micro-radio as a learning tool to begin a career in radio, or developing a networked system of micro-radios to expand the range of existing projects.

Regardless of the broadcast range one is working with, there is considerable debate on whether to choose a vacant band location on the dial or stepping into the band location of an existing radio station, a tactic used in order to borrow the larger listenership of a

sure did with the construction of TAR. After two weeks, my self-taught course in electronics was completed. There before me sat TAR, my newly completed radio station. I looked at this item, about three-by-one inches, looked at the various components sticking out of it—all of which I had painstakingly soldered onto this tiny circuit board—and realized that at long last, it was time to tune TAR onto the FM band. Of course, doubts about the functional ability of the transmitter overwhelmed my brain, but my mule-like nature pushed me forward and a two-day bout of tuning began.

Besides the radio transmitter itself, I had made a dipole antenna, stolen from an unused television set (I've always

commercial station. As broadcast range increases, these debates become more important. Despite scare-tactic information, the Canadian Radio-Television and Telecommunications Commission (CRTC) does not generally interfere with micro- or pirate radio broadcasters unless they have received complaints. These complaints arise from commercial broadcasters who have had their signal overridden by a pirate.

During Seattle's World Trade Organization convention and popular uprising in 1999, there were a number of micro, pirate, and community radio stations working to provide coverage of the battle on the streets from a grassroots perspective. The pirate radio collective, Voices of Occupied Seattle, spent time pasting flyers and stickers around the downtown area that listed local available FM frequencies. Broadcasts came out of Free Radio Seattle and the pirate station Y2WTKO, transmitted from a tree on the Olympic Peninsula. It was also imported online by Eugene, Oregon's Radio Free Cascadia collective.[8] Individuals involved wore broadcasting equipment under their clothing in order to broadcast via high points in the city. In other instances, cell phones were used to get up-to-the-minute reports on what was happening on the ground. Individuals used suitcase transmitters with umbrella antennas to broadcast within the protest itself. Free Radio Seattle linked up to Radio X to stream live audio content via the internet.

lantern batteries in series as a power source. Slowly but
surely, through sheer persistence, I began to hear the
beginnings of TAR trickling through my radio. A friend was
quickly brought onboard, allowing me to hang off my balcony,
pushing my low-tech antenna mounted on a broom handle
further out into the cosmos. She listened at the radio,
shouting out encouragement as the clarity began to improve.
With all the shouting, jumping, and back patting, one would
think a new baby had arrived. And indeed, TAR was born
right here on 90.7 FM on a brisk autumn day in Montréal.
TAR was on the air. TAR is back on the air today. Listen up.

The results varied. Due to a lack of communication between independent organizations, efforts were not always consolidated but rather divided. On one occasion, Free Radio Seattle was bumped up the band by Y2WTKO because of discrepancies with locations on the dial. Yet, the advantage of so many approaches was that news was coming out of a number of pirate sources. In some cases, the transmission range was fairly extensive because it was picked up by pirate radio stations or streamed over the internet. In other cases, broadcasts were not making it out of the protest zone. Despite criticism of the anti-WTO uprising and popular movements in general, the ability to offer up revolutionary, alternative, and autonomous media is alive and on-going. The people involved continue to experiment, and together, these experiments are catalysts for social awareness and change.

The *Radio Libertad* project is one recent example of media solidarity between activists in Montréal and Indigenous communities in Guerrero, Mexico.[9] Individuals within this alliance recognize issues of inequality in terms of access to technological resources, and activists in Canada offer help in the form of fundraising efforts, training, and information dissemination. The *Radio Libertad* project has been undertaken primarily by the *Organización Independiente de Pueblos Mixteco y Tlapaneco* (OIPMT) in Mexico and strives to supply an autonomous community radio station to the Mixteco and Tlapaneco peoples in order to combat the prevalent political and military repression.

COME AND GET IT. GO AND DO IT

Are you motivated yet? TAR provides an autonomous and alternative radio experience. The size, range, method of construction, reliance on friends, spontaneous and organized call for contributors to come forward with self-defined alternative content, and transitory nature of TAR have all contributed to a vibrant, positive environment. And above all, this is only a beginning. We have limited times of broadcast, limited range, a small audience, but it is the act of doing that is essential. TAR creates a sense of community that emerges out of the live process. From here, the options are endless.

Despite confiscation of equipment and the disappearances of activists across Mexico, *Radio Libertad* is moving forward, joining the over 400 free radio stations across Mexico, working to maintain Indigenous rights and culture. *Radio Libertad* is an example of autonomous radio being built in a location where there is little to no infrastructure for radio. Because it is operated by community members, community issues are put at the forefront with informational broadcasts and organizing tactics. Within its context, it is an important move, that will provide a viable media alternative to government sponsored media. Solidarity between activists in Montréal and the OIPMT provides the advantage of sharing economic resources to fund and create the station. The collaboration also allows *Radio Libertad* to have a greater chance of success by informing a potential international audience—through webcasting and information dissemination on behalf of the Montréal chapter—of the issues of repression faced by the peoples from the Mexican state of Guerrero. As was illustrated by the media efforts of the Zapatistas in Chiapas, Mexico, over the past 15 years, global alliances are crucially important for resisting state-sponsored injustices, and working towards self-determination.

The use of radio for activist pursuits takes many forms, thus allowing for the development and overlapping of a number of tactics and approaches to radical media that affect individuals and communities, both locally and globally. Media can be structured around personal engagement and

In the long-term future, TAR will continue to pop up and build an audience of contributors and listeners. They will continue to transform their lives and link together in a new community. Today, this is only one beginning for TAR. Temporary Autonomous Radio is only one small example out of the endless radio opportunities available to us all.

You've been listening to TAR on 90.7 FM. Coming up next is the ever infamous, radio karaoke. First song up: get ready for it... Rage Against the Machine and Guerrilla Radio.[10]

concern for the struggles of others, rather than solely for economic benefits. Temporary autonomous radio permits tactical information and dissenting opinions to be disseminated, provides individual empowerment, and room for the silenced to speak. A more permanent autonomous radio facilitates collective memory, promotes radio activism to more people, and creates communities and networks passionate about access to public airwaves.

The challenge is to continue imagining and unearthing revolutionary, radical, autonomous, spontaneous, creative ways of accessing the airwaves and filling them with the voices of many.

notes

[1] For more on Temporary Autonomous Zones, read: Bey, Hakim. (1991) : *The Temporary Autonomous Zone, Ontological Anarchy, Poetic Terrorism*. New York: Autonomedia. Published online at: http://www.flashback.se/archive/taz/ [accessed June 1, 2004].

[2] Walker, Jesse. (2001). *Rebels on the Air: An Alternative History of Radio in America*. New York: New York University Press.

[3] McChesney, Robert W. "The Battle for the U.S. Airwaves, 1928-1935," *Journal of Communication*. Vol. 40 (4), Autumn 1990, pgs. 29-57.

[4] Brecht, Bertolt. (1979). "Radio as a Means of Communication: A Talk of the Function of Radio (Germany, 1930)," *Communication and Class Struggle*. Vol. 2, Mattelart, Armand & Seth Siegelaub (eds.). New York: International General, pgs. 169-171.

[5] King, Gretchen. (October 2004). Micro-radio, pirate radio, and community radio activist. Personal Interview.

[6] Hockheimer, John L. "Organizing Democratic Radio: Issues of Practice," *Media, Culture and Society*, Vol. 15, No.3, July 1993.

[7] For the full case-study of Tetsuo Kogawa's Tokyo experience, check out: Kogawa, Tetsuo. (1994). "Toward Polymorphous Radio," *Radio Rethink: Art, Sound and Transmission*. Banff: Walter Phillips Gallery, pgs. 287-300.

[8] The full history of Radio Cascadia, as told by miscreant. Published online at: http://riseup.net/radiofreecascadia/y2wtko/aural.htm [accessed November 12, 2004].

[9] Ahooja, Sarita. (October 2004). Activist with *Radio Libertad*. Personal email interview.

[10] The audio version of this segment of "Broadcasting on Our Own Terms" can be heard at http://www.cumuluspress.com

web resources

Pirate Radio Caroline: www.radiocaroline.co.uk
Radio for All: www.radio4all.org
Radio Free Cascadia: www.riseup.net/radiofreecascadia
Radio X: www.radiox.wirerimmed.com
Y2WTKO: www.riseup.net/radiofreecascadia/y2wtko

IS OPEN?

"Media everywhere information nowhere!" is a little used, yet poignant, slogan cried out at large demos where the cameras and journalists of corporate media are omnipresent but in-depth coverage of social justice issues is not. Embodied in this slogan is the common belief among activists that the corporate-run mass media present obstacles to social justice movements. Although some groups have found ways to get their messages into the mainstream media, whether through the staging of media attention grabbing spectacles or the funnelling of resources into media relations, many groups experience media coverage that shows their actions through a distorted lens. For the 1999 protests against the World Trade Organization (WTO), activists in Seattle decided to flip this dynamic, crying out: "Don't hate the media, be the media." And with this summersault, the Independent Media Centre, Indymedia (IMC) was born.

What most think of now when they think of Indymedia is the network of websites, but the IMC actually started as a physical space for alternative and independent media-makers to gather during the protests in Seattle. The IMC website served as a newswire for protesters and independent journalists, accessible through the computers at the centre. The network of websites that it has become can trace its beginning to a chance encounter between an Australian media activist and one of the Seattle IMC organizers one month prior to the Seattle anti-WTO demonstrations. As documented by Scott Uzelman in his work on Indymedia Vancouver,[1] the activist from Australia convinced the web designers to adopt open source software designed by Community Activist Technology that would allow the public to upload content to the site. The software fit with the activists' vision of the project because it allowed decentralized media production and content sharing. Whereas traditional website creation and maintenance requires a centralized webmaster or webmistress to upload and organize information, the open publishing software allowed users from any computer to upload, organize, and download the multimedia content.

On a practical level, open publishing[2] software permitted the decentralization of work among many media activists and independent journalists. On an ideological level, it allowed activists to move away from a centralized mass media model, where a few people decide what content is important, to a horizontal, decentralized model based on collaboration and reciprocity. Through the Indymedia project, the puzzle pieces of political ideas and of technology snapped into place. Everyone with internet access and basic skills was now able to contribute to the creation of news, whether they were based in Europe, South Africa, the U.S.A., or directly at the IMC. This new form of access to publishing was very new at the time, and represented a huge advancement in the way the internet was used, although, admittedly, the digital divide and literacy issues remain obstacles for much of the world's population.

The result was what has come to be known as open publishing, a practice in which the process of creating the content is transparent to the readers and that they too can get involved, either by writing articles, or by setting up their own site. All content is copyleft, meaning that anyone is free to take and use it for non-profit purposes so long as they give credit to the original author. In open publishing anyone can be a media manipulator. Also implicit is the principle of reciprocity—a concept which cyber-theorist Pierre Lévy sees as integral to virtual communities. According to Lévy, reciprocity in this context means that if we learn something from the information exchanged, we are expected to share information that could be of use to someone else.[3] With open publishing, the historical divide between producer and consumer is narrowed, although, it must be acknowledged, never eliminated completely because of issues around access to technology and the knowledge needed to use it, which is one of the major critiques of Indymedia.

Indymedia collectives centre their work on the philosophy of open publishing as they seek to create a free information network, based on a democratic model of production and distribution, in which the content available is exchanged horizontally from user to user, media-producer to media-producer, activist to activist. The technology that enables open publishing was created within the open source software movement, which was founded on the value of equal access to free information. Once this technology was officially in the hands of media activists located in the global justice movement, it was then moulded and further developed to fit activists' needs and philosophies.

The point is that, although it may seem as though the software technology influenced the structure of the IMC, it is not the technology which determined what would be done, but rather the activists who formed and developed technology to fit their needs and values. It is therefore important to think about open publishing as a theory, or philosophy, which is put into practice, rather than as a technology that determines how the Indymedia network develops. The practice of open publishing can be seen, then, as reflecting the principles of the movement—democracy, reciprocity, free access to information, and collective action.

indymedia as an alternative space online

The Indymedia network provides a space online in which open publishing can be used to promote dialogue and communication instead of one-way dissemination. Within these carved out alternative spaces, activists can—to borrow the words of Andrew Wood and Andrew Smith—use "computer networks to construct discursive resistance to dominant forces—to build alternative paths, hiding places, impromptu monuments, and unauthorized meeting places online."[4] Every time someone publishes something on an Indymedia site, they are engaging in the active production of media and are also opening themselves up to feedback on their observations and analysis through the commentary function. They are participating in a space where some of the barriers to access with regards to media production are eliminated—a space where the politics of speech (i.e., whose voice is legitimate) found in mainstream society are challenged, along with the commodification of information, and state control of communication networks.

There are many benefits to these types of spaces that strive to embody the alternatives that they propose. This embodiment can be defined as activism that seeks to criticize the dominant social order or to engage with it, while also attempting to create something new. However, despite the accomplishments possible within these types of spaces, there can come a time when the problems associated with the structures of capitalism and patriarchy find their way inside.

When it comes to Indymedia, because it is a media space where people discuss global social justice issues, various forms of discrimination, such as sexism, racism, and homophobia, are often addressed. The intentions of the activists and groups linked with Indymedia are specifically not to ignore that inequality and oppression exist. What Indymedia activists have sought to do is to create a space where these issues can be discussed, uncovered, and where strategies and solutions can be presented. Open publishing seeks to give people equal access to a space for dialogue and information sharing.

Yet as the Indymedia network mushroomed into an expansive global network made up of close to 100 autonomous collectives, it became clear that inequality, homophobia, sexism, racism, anti-Semitism, and other forms of discrimination, as well as disrespect for the principles behind the project, had found their way onto the websites. Within the Indymedia collectives, which organize horizontally and make decisions through consensus, this manifests itself as power imbalances relating to gender, race, sexual orientation, class, and knowledge about technology. These have presented challenges on an organizational level. Another way that this manifests, which this chapter will explore, is the occurrence of postings to the newswire that reproduce systems of oppression.

the development of open publishing policies

> The ideal of creating a media source that would be totally inclusive has had to endure tremendous tests. Open publishing, the purest form of the idea, has become, in some instances, Indymedia's greatest liability.
>
> — Gal Beckerman[5]

Many Indymedia collectives, after experiencing abuses such as postings ranging from spam, to pornography and hate-mongering, decided to develop editorial policies for their sites. For most collectives, this took the form of a policy statement which outlined the collective's right to filter the newswire's content and the guidelines used to do this. Some collectives, such as Québec Indymedia (CMAQ), have developed software that supports a validation process, where, once submitted, all articles go to a waiting place (which is accessible to all registered users) until they are validated by a member of the validation committee and published in the newswire.

Most Indymedia collectives started out without editorial policies and a complete openness with regards to content. Because most of these collectives formed with a particular event in mind, such as covering the summits of the World Trade Organization or G8, their initial content revolved around coverage of these events. As well, the Indymedia Global "Principles of Unity" positions IMCs within movements struggling for the right to communicate and to share information. IMCs are also organized around the principle of human equality, and their principles of unity state that they shall not discriminate and that they are committed to building diversity within their localities. These strong statements, along with those associated within the philosophy of open publishing outlined above, situate Indymedia as a network and autonomous media project that operates with the goal of actively addressing inequality. The value of freedom of speech is also central to Indymedia. Yet the commitment to addressing

51

inequality and diverse oppressions as well as promoting participatory communication has presented some challenges to Indymedia collectives.

An article by Gal Beckerman in the COLUMBIA JOURNALISM REVIEW exposes some of these challenges. According to Beckerman, New York Indymedia developed editorial policies after their site was deluged with posts that had nothing to do with the struggles of the global justice movement—anti-Semitic rants, racist caricatures, and pornography all competed, democratically, for space on the wire. This is a story common to many IMCs. Many collectives do not develop editorial policies until a situation arises that threatens collective members' (or sometimes non-collective members') vision of what is acceptable on the newswire.

The editorial policies developed by Indymedia collectives are for the most part quite similar to one another in their inclusion of a section outlining the guiding principles of the policy. An example from Seattle Indymedia reads that the purpose of Seattle Indymedia is to provide an unmoderated, open-publishing newswire in accordance with established IMC policies and philosophy; to maintain the newswire and website as a community space, and a safe environment for users, especially members of disempowered or marginalized groups; to acknowledge that speech has the power to cause injury, but that instances of injurious speech should also be seen as opportunities for insurrectionary response; and, to preserve the quality of the website as a useful media resource. With these guiding principles in mind, the second half of the policy outlines that collectives reserve the right to reclassify material on the website, which may mean choosing to highlight it in the centre column, to bundle it together with several postings on the same topic, or to place it in a "hidden" folder. Posts that are hidden without debate are those which are duplicates of articles on the site, advertisements for jobs or consumer items, or posts that have no content in them.

Some collectives interpret the last of these more broadly than others. For some, no content means literally a blank posting or only links to another site, whereas other collectives hide material that is devoid of comprehensible material (a bad resolution photo or a rant that has no obvious point). Most collectives agree that there shall be no editing whatsoever of a post, unless requested by the author.

These policies were all developed with much discussion and debate and are continuously placed under scrutiny. Central to the editorial policies of each collective is the principle of transparency. Measures that guarantee that the moderating process is transparent are central to Indymedia collectives because they are based on a critique of the news selection traditions of mainstream media. In order to be transparent, collective members engage in discussions over editorial listservs before removing a post, write statements as to why a post was hidden, and, if possible, send an email to the person who submitted the post explaining why it was moved or hidden. The editorial policy and all decisions made through it are always open to debate within collectives and from those not involved within the collective. For many collectives this process is one that involves personal reflection as well. The following question is often asked: Do I want to hide this post because I do not agree with its content or because it violates the editorial policy?

Many of the posts that Indymedia collectives decide to moderate are hidden either because they contain discriminatory, libellous content, or use language that encourages hate and violence. Although this may seem straightforward in terms of what content should not be on the site, in at least three cases, it is not.

First, Indymedia websites are supposed to be a space for dialogue on social problems. Racism and other behaviours exist in our society and some people believe that suppressing them will not make them disappear. Instead, why not use the "add comment" function on the site to spark a debate on the offensive posting as opposed to removing the posting from the newswire? Some collectives choose to leave this material on the main pages of the site in order to allow discussions to happen. This tactic seems to work if this type of content is only submitted occasionally, but in the cases of New York, Québec, and Paris Indymedia sites, among others, the amount of racist and/or sexist postings became so pervasive on their newswires that more vigilant filtering was required. Furthermore, the principles of unity, as mentioned above, state that Indymedia collectives seek to address inequalities. If the newswire propagates sexist and racist points of view, can Indymedia be seen as promoting diversity and equality? This is a question that collectives have had to answer when determining whether it is necessary or desirous to narrow the content of the site.

Secondly, it is not always extremely clear whether a posting is, for example, sexist. With the case of Québec Indymedia, which involved an extensive flooding of their site with anti-feminist, sexist, and defamatory postings, the sexism found within the articles was at times subtle, yet present. This made editorial decisions difficult for the collective, partially because of the time-consuming process of moderating so many offensive postings. As well, the collective had to decide whether to block all postings from the offending individuals (who after count-  less requests would not stop posting many articles and comments, daily to the newswire). They decided instead that it was important to judge the posting as to whether it was unacceptable, regardless of who submitted it. The offending individual kept posting sexist and defamatory remarks, to the point that he was symbolically banned from Québec Indymedia's site, a step that was taken along with other strict editorial policy changes.

The metaphor of the slippery slope often comes up with Indymedia collectives with regards to moderating their sites. It is a metaphor that envelops the fear involved in making decisions as to what constitutes valid content—first a blatantly hateful article is hidden, then one that is less blatant, and so on, until the collectives are left making judgements on the nuances of texts. It also begs the question of the political orientation of the website—is it only a site for global justice activists and their points of view, or is it a democratic public space where all points of view are welcome? Is Indymedia responsible for promoting free speech at all costs? To whom are they accountable—those wishing to express hate-filled views or those who suffer the consequences of such views?

Lastly, in some cases there can be no debate as to whether a post is made completely inaccessible to the general public because of legal issues. In countries like Canada, it is illegal to publish hate speech, child pornography, or libellous material (Sections 318 and 319 of the Canadian

Criminal Code). Therefore collectives within Canada need to be vigilant about content on their site, for the sake of their member's legal protection. As well, the abundance of copyright laws and the many cases being waged for the protection of intellectual property make it necessary for collectives to screen content to the best of their abilities to ensure that the content is not copyrighted. Even though Indymedia sites have a disclaimer that says that they are not responsible for the content on the site and that it does not necessarily represent the views of the collective, collectives (in Canada at least) could be held legally responsible for illegal content.

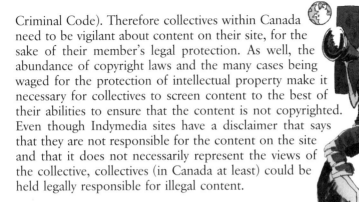

rights, responsibility, and accountability

With the exercise of power, comes responsibility. For Indymedia collectives, the adoption of editorial policies also meant that they were creating a system where they would have the power to judge what is and what is not appropriate content for the site. Their discomfort in developing these policies is therefore understandable in that Indymedia was created to promote participatory communication and to provide a space for views that are otherwise not published. With the introduction of policies defining which points of view are acceptable also come new levels of responsibility. Those filtering the content on the site are now responsible for reading all postings, identifying problematic material, and engaging in a discussion with their editorial committees as to what to do with that material. There is also the need to make this process transparent, as discussed above.

The editorial policies have also brought the issue of accountability to the surface. Collective members become even more accountable to their collaborators (those who read and post to the site) after establishing editorial policies. On the one hand, those who post to the site have a right to know that their post was hidden and why. On the other hand, readers may want the right to see this rejected content (which is usually linked to the editorial policy) and may hold collective members accountable if inappropriate content makes it onto the site.

The second of these has occurred with Québec and Paris Indymedia, both of which have been chastised and pressured from social justice groups regarding the content of their site. In the case of the large amount of sexist material being posted to the Québec site, there were not only the offending users to deal with, but also a small group of feminists who were putting extreme pressures on the collective. These individual feminists were upset by the publishing of anything coming from identified masculin‑ists (the term used to describe a specific anti‑feminist, sexist movement), whether the material was blatantly sexist or not. They showed their frustration by using pressure tactics, such as a call for a boycott of the site to push Indymedia members to block all offending users from their site, make all hidden posts inaccessible to the public, and shut down the comment function completely.

Similarly, last year, Paris Indymedia was declared "irresponsible" in a public letter written by an anarchist group (*Alternative libertaire*) because of some racist content on their site. This anarchist group suggests that open publishing is irresponsible because it allows racist and colonialist discourses on the site. They also make suggestions on how Paris Indymedia should deal with this issue.

As these two cases illustrate, there seems to be a transposition of the notion of responsibility with regards to content found in traditional media onto that found on Indymedia. When readers are upset about content found on the sites, they tend to blame the collectives behind the Indymedia and write a type of letter to the editor which includes a threat to end their subscription, so to speak. The involvement of collaborators in suggesting improvements to the site is not unwanted by Indymedia collectives, as their principles of unity state that they are open to anyone and that the editorial process is open to scrutiny. And just as some people criticize Indymedia for the content that remains in the newswire, there are also many critiques waged by those who feel that they have experienced censorship.

towards new conceptions of "open"

Even with editorial policies in place, the process of open publishing is never straightforward, but is instead a constant process of negotiation, with its triumphs and failures. As this chapter illustrates, the most significant

obstacle faced by Indymedia collectives in developing policies around open publishing is the balancing of strong values, such as openness and responsibility. The development of editorial policies, such as those outlined above, has placed Indymedia collectives in the role of mediator—a role that can be confining and limiting.

The strong point of this is that it forces collectives to take on this role actively and accountably. Whereas before the development of formal policy some collectives engaged in editing of the site in ways that may not have been so transparent, the editorial policies place these activities front and centre in a public document. It is therefore clear how each collective defines open publishing and what their vision is on hate-filled material. On the down side, editorial policies have also loaded work onto the backs of already burdened volunteers. With accountability comes work. If an editorial policy states what types of material are not permitted on the site, it is up to the collectives to ensure that these policies are enacted. In some cases, this extra work load has limited collectives' abilities to take on more projects. The website that supports a movement thus becomes a liability in terms of resources (e.g., people's un-paid time).

Despite the difficulties in dealing with these challenges, the development of editorial policies has no doubt strengthened the Indymedia network. It has pushed the limits of open publishing, stimulated the development of new tools within open source software, and created an opportunity for collectives to better define their purpose and their vision of Indymedia. The need to push open publishing forward is not a liability, but a strength. As Robert McChesney, an American media theorist and political economist, says, "the Indymedia movement is not obliged to be a movement for every point of view under the sun. They need to make tough editorial decisions, and that's not something to be despondent about. The problem is not that you have to make decisions. The important thing is that you make them based on principles that are transparent."[6]

Indymedia has been placed under scrutiny, as the Québec and Paris examples show, pushing members to answer difficult questions about the practice of open publishing. In some cases, this has led to the development of new software tools that make the process more transparent, that allow the collaborators to get involved, and that decentralize the editorial process. In an article entitled THREE PROPOSALS FOR OPEN PUBLISHING, Dru Oja Jay outlines some possibilities, from "filters" to "rating systems," which allow users to rate content and thus take part in deciding which content should be highlighted on the site.[7] Other non-Indymedia initiatives, such as the Creative Commons project, attempt to build on the concept of copyleft, creating a more complex and nuanced understanding of information owning and sharing. Yet other projects, such as the Indymedia Radio Network, build on ideas of open publishing using other media, thus breaking down technological barriers.

These are just a few of the possibilities in the future of open publishing. What is important at this point is that we move beyond the unquestioning celebration of Indymedia as a revolutionary example and into public debates about some of the issues that threaten its foundations as an autonomous medium. It is through these discussions that open publishing theory and practice will continue to provide insights as to what a democratic and participatory media environment looks like.

notes

Previous versions of this essay were published in *GR Journal For The Arts, Sciences & Technology* (Vol. 2, No. 1) and Open Journal http://openj.touchbasic.com. A special thanks to Leslie Regan Shade for her feedback and encouragement.

[1] Uzelman, Scott. (2002). *Catalyzing Participatory Communication: Independent Media Centre and the Politics of Direct Action*. Unpublished Master's thesis: Simon Fraser University. Published online at: http://ender/indymedia.org/twiki/bin/view/vancouver/historyofvanimc [accessed October 22, 2003].

[2] Matthew Arnison, one of the developers of IMC software, suggests a working definition of open publishing: "Open publishing means that the process of creating news is transparent to the readers. They can contribute a story and see it appear instantly in the pool of stories publicly available. Those stories are filtered as little as possible to help the readers find the stories they want. Readers can see editorial decisions being made by others. They can see how to get involved and help make editorial decisions. If they can think of a better way for the software to help shape editorial decisions, they can copy the software because it is free and change it and start their own site. If they want to redistribute the news, they can, preferably on an open publishing site." See: http://www.sarai.net/journal/02PDF/10infopol/10open_publishing.pdf

[3] Lévy, Pierre. (2001). *Cyberculture*. (Translated by Robert Bononno) Minneapolis: University of Minnesota Press.

[4] Wood, Andrew F., & Matthew J. Smith. (2001). *Online Communication: Linking Technology, Identity, and Culture*. London, U.K.: Lawrence Erlbaum Associates, Publishers.

[5] Beckerman, Gal. (2003). "Edging Away from Anarchy: Inside the Indymedia Collective, Passion vs. Pragmatism," *Columbia Journalism Review*, Issue 5. Published online at: http://www.cjr.org/issues/2003/5/anarchy-beckerman.asp [accessed October 22, 2003].

[6] McChesney, Robert quoted in Becherman, Gal. (2003).

[7] Jay, Dru Oja. (n.d.). "Three Proposals for Open Publishing." Published online at: http://dru.ca/imc/open_pub.html [accessed October 22, 2003].

web resources

Community Activist Technology: www.cat.org.au
Creative Commons: www.creativecommons.org
Indymedia: www.indymedia.org
Indymedia Radio Network: radio.indymedia.org
Zombie: zombie.lautre.net

are you: creative?
got time on your hands?
disenchanted with consumer culture?
looking for a fun way to bite the hand that feeds you?
try culture jamming, a favoured new pastime of budding revolutionaries everywhere! stop bitching about your culture and make it your playground, make its icons your palette. turn all your nasty frustration into public art! you'll be glad you did!

the unclassifiable force

Rising in close tandem with our beloved consumer culture, a new resistant strain of dissidence has come to occupy a special, if confusing, place in discussions around art, media activism, and politics. In the discourse around autonomous media, culture jamming is, in marketing terms, a "tweener". Neither this nor that, it doesn't fit nicely into any box and cannot be classified readily as a medium of communication.

Though countercultural, culture jamming shadows and heavily references mainstream media icons, especially those of advertising. Though it is often created autonomously, it can also be produced by established NGOs. It can be executed with a marker (on an ad). It can also be created with high-end editing equipment (a TV "anti-ad"). To some it is a tactical form of activist communication. To others, it is a cultural practice—a personal way of acting out that helps moderate the tensions of living in a society that largely does not reflect their social and environmental values.

what is culture jamming anyways?

Most people have seen spoofs of corporate logos or mock-ups of official websites, altered billboards or "Starfucks" stickers. Some may have heard of elaborate pranks, involving the impersonation of World Trade Organization officials during conferences in Italy and Finland or the 1998 grand opening of the "No Shop" in London, set up to sell nothing. Given that each of these may be considered acts of culture jamming, what is the unifying thread that ties them together?

Culture jamming is cultural backtalk, using the language of established power. The practice is subversive by nature. It is about playing with familiar forms of communication and interaction (posters, billboards, official language, protocol, spaces) and imagery (logos, ad spreads, official documents) and turning them back against the culture that created them. A subverted message may be a critique of the original, like the cigarette giant's ad mascot, Joe Camel transformed into a terminally ill "Joe Chemo". A subverted sign may also piggyback a new political message, such as "Class War: Just Do It". Culture jamming can be done quick-and-dirty with a marker on an ad. It can equally involve the creation of slick media, requiring the sophistication of elaborate graphic design and copy writing.

a brief history of jamming

Culture jamming brings a contemporary twist to a long legacy of court jesting, political satire, and playful disruptions of the social order. Unlike its predecessors, though, this contemporary subversive game is played predominantly with symbols and signs in a society that has come to be permeated with them.

The stage for the emergence of culture jamming was set in the beginning of the 20th century as mass production, mass consumption, and mass transportation became established in Europe and North America. The acceleration that accompanied these new developments created an avalanche of information, and industrial societies had to seek out and develop more efficient codes of communication to deal with it all. These factors made symbolic languages more important than ever and gave rise to many new symbolic codes from road map icons to corporate logos, all designed to make quick sense of increasingly complex information. As these languages multiplied, Western cultures, their views of themselves, and their very sense of reality came to rely on the use of symbols as never before.

From the worlds of art and academia, reactions to this new order of signs came quickly. In the early part of the 20th century, artists of the Dada and Surrealist movements made their mark by manipulating symbols and turning visual reality on its head with their creations. Seeing everyday objects recast in absurd contexts, the viewing public got an early taste of the power of the subverted image. In the 1950s and '60s, a network of renegade European artists and intellectuals calling themselves Situationists, gave this artistic practice a name and a mission: *détournement*. They proposed it as a tactic with revolutionary political potential. If reality is made up of signs, they argued, then we have only to turn the signs around to change the society we live in.

Yet, culture jamming is not just about art and academia. It has always also been a scruffy child of the streets. While it was being discussed in ivory towers, there were important pioneers who were "just doing it" in their urban environments. As early as the 1930s, there are records of people walking up to roadside ads and altering them to suit their tastes. In the countercultural 1960s, Yippies were beginning to practice symbolic warfare, like raining dollar bills down on the trading floor to disrupt the New York Stock Exchange. The Billboard Liberation Front—children of the 1970s—have been perfecting the art of high-impact billboard alteration ever since. Activist artists of the 1980s and early '90s, like Barbara Kruger, have made the subversive billboard an art form in itself.

In the past two decades, culture jamming has caught-on far and wide, thanks to the growing reach of alternative media, the accessibility of digital design tools, and the vast social and activist networks now linked by the internet. Sharing newsstand shelf space with HOME AND GARDEN and WALLPAPER across the world since 1990, ADBUSTERS MAGAZINE has been bringing culture jammed images into the mainstream like no one else has.

Since image manipulation and graphic design software have been in the hands of millions of non-professional designers, subverting images or ads has become child's play. What's more, digital image-based culture jams now find their way around the web and into our email inboxes with great facility.

a global virus

The phenomenon of globalization is also doing its part to internationalize subversion along with big-box stores and other modern goodies. One thing is certain: culture jamming is a catchy tactic. It seems that wherever consumer culture sets down roots, culture jamming techniques are quick to appear.

Though culture jamming had its beginnings in the European and North American art world, it has recently taken root in many countries around the globe. There is something very seductive about the ability to respond to all the noise that consumer culture surrounds us with. Social networks have linked cultures so closely that a clever practice on one continent can be quickly adopted on another the next day. The phenomenal spread of The Media Foundation's Buy Nothing Day campaign is such an example. The idea is to pick a date in November and create an anti-event: a focal point of protest against over-consumption. The idea started in Vancouver in the early 1990s and, with some promotion and a minimal budget, it has been autonomously undertaken and organized by culture jammers in over 50 countries.

Interestingly, a new convergence point of autonomous culture jamming has sprung up in Slovenia where consumer culture is still something of a novelty. In 2001, when I was an employee of Adbusters Media Foundation, I was invited to present the foundations' vision of culture jamming at an advertising conference in Maribor. There I came upon a group of culture jamming enthusiasts. These young Slovenians had grown up in a country that had shifted gears rapidly from state socialism to consumer capitalism in ten short years. They were eager to challenge and question their new status quo. Though much of the culture jamming they were seeing came from other cultural contexts, they were quick to see how it could be adapted to the current Slovenian context.

One of these jamming shit-disturbers, Oliver Vodeb, launched Memefest, an International Festival of Radical Communication. Unlike

ADBUSTERS, which mainly publishes its own creations, Memefest's main purpose is to encourage and showcase grassroots culture jams from Slovenia and around the world. It has become a culture jamming academy that brings exposure to jammed messages and gives each participant public feedback on how to refine their message and style.

Year after year, the crop of submissions to Memefest gets bigger and, interestingly, much of it comes from countries where advertising and consumer culture are quite new. The culture jams from a diversity of countries have provided an interesting window for seeing how individuals from different cultures are reacting to the global phenomenon of consumer capitalism. Though many of the culture jams in Memefest are not as polished as those put together by established players, such as The Media Foundation, it is encouraging to see the sheer volume of creativity from around the world because from their different starting points, young subversives are taking back some power to express their culture for themselves. Every time they manipulate a corporate logo or comment on their surroundings, using the visual language of advertising, they chip away at the untouchable aura of the new consumer capitalist system and realize that culture is something that they can actively influence.

what do we make of culture jamming today?

Being an odd kid-on-the-block, culture jamming often raises controversy and questions from all sides of the political spectrum and it is especially criticized by activists of the Left. Since it is so linked to the icons of capitalist culture, it is seen as suspect by some in anti-capitalist movements. They may ask the valid question: "Can something that grows out of the mainstream possibly serve to change it?" Many others are put-off by the mischief and playfulness inherent in culture jamming. They think it makes light of serious issues. But then, why should the element of play be incompatible with fighting for a better world? Culture jamming also has its share of wild-eyed proponents who believe it is a new self-contained approach to activism that will succeed where, in their minds, the outdated tactics of the Left have failed. What it takes, according to them, is a critical mass of people culture jamming at the same time to disrupt the mass media spectacle and eventually derail current consumer culture.

I am somewhat ambivalent about culture jamming's relevance as a political phenomenon. However, I have

developed, through experience, a personal lens for evaluating the effects of culture jamming in different contexts. It is helpful to view culture jamming as an empowering cultural practice rather than a type of media or a form of communication. As a practice, it is largely shaped by individuals who often work in small affinity groups and negotiate a critical path through the modern mediascape.

In this context, the playful and subversive manipulation of mainstream symbols is most meaningful to the culture jammer herself and the group involved in the jamming. By appropriating and manipulating mainstream symbols, the culture jammer cuts the monolithic authority of consumer culture down to size, and gains a certain sense of personal control over it. It is the process of subverting a billboard, creating a mock corporate website, or lampooning consumer behaviour that is empowering and can lead to a larger appetite for other social change initiatives. When culture jamming is used as a vehicle to carry a message to others, some of this transformative effect is lost. After all, as much as the recipients of a pre-packaged message can enjoy the wit of the finished product, they have not taken part in the appropriation and alteration of that message.

caution: jammers at work

you've started by altering a few tiresome ads with a marker, with some stickers. now, you have a mind to post some slicker messages of your own around town, to push back against the consumer current. you walk through your city differently these days, your critical eye scanning the visual environment. the concrete, the prefab, and the ads that get you down are no longer things that suck. they've become things that need fixing.

months later, you're in the elevator of a major office tower, going floor to floor disguised as a bike courier, delivering self-published notices of corporate misdoing. you realize you're just as stressed as the office types around you. after all, posting these subversive forms is risky and demanding work.

another time, you're climbing up a billboard to do some editing and you get the shakes. some of your usual doubts jump to centre stage: why are you doing this? will you get caught this time? is this some

stupid stunt or a brave act of defiance? will this change minds or just piss people off? too late. you're already slapping up your message before you can help yourself.

you just can't go back to being a consumer, grumbling about the offerings. you've become an addicted cultural producer that meets in bars every week with a like-minded gang of malcontents. your creations are pranks, public art projects, and guerrilla communications campaigns. you've never felt so powerful, productive, and alive.

I have been involved with culture jamming on many different levels but the grassroots street-level adventures I had with the Public Works collective in Vancouver—and a similar short-lived group in Montréal—were, to me, the real deal. Both collectives started with friends and friends of friends who came together out of a shared sense that we lived in cities out of balance. Advertising had grabbed too much of the public space, crowding our consciousness with sexism, greed, empty values—basically, with crap. Our meetings were not discussion groups where we would moan about the status quo. Those that answered the call to form the groups were looking to get busy and do something about their cultural environment. Pronto.

We met regularly in cheap bars. To start we made our shit list, a rundown of the things around town that were pissing us off, like omnipresent ad campaigns, or municipal issues that needed public attention. Next, we would embark on the creative level of our meetings by having a campaign brainstorm session much like you would find at an advertising firm. Ideas would be bounced around for a main message to convey in our jams, then we would discuss the medium, be it a website, street performance, or fridge magnet. Near the end, we broke the task down and arranged a schedule during the following week to pull it off. Then, once the organizing was out of the way, the evening could happily degenerate into silliness and debauchery.

Over time, life in the collective took on a comfortable rhythm. Some projects had weeks of preparation, during which we pulled-off a few quick jams—some SUV bumper-stickering, some environmental violation notices on car windshields, or other small gestures to keep us tied to the energy of action. That was our magic recipe. In one meeting, we would identify

what we saw was wrong, plan out a course of attack, and, within a week or two, have done something about it. Our goals were short term, our rewards were immediate, and we rarely had enough time to bicker.

As a whole, our work ended up being quite diverse. We did alter a couple of billboards and made posters, stickers, and stencils to post around town. We liked to vary our medium as often as possible, to keep things interesting. Over time, we came up with some innovative ways of getting a message across. For example, we installed retractable curtains on bus shelter advertisements in Vancouver, and sculpted a spoof ad snow sculpture looking onto a popular outdoor skating rink in Montréal.

Some of our jams were more involved. For one action, we produced slick Corporate Charter Revocation Notices bearing the names of offending corporations and then posted them in the elevators of their corporate headquarters and in elevators of the Vancouver Stock Exchange. The following summer, we unloaded a truck full of sod on Vancouver's trendy Commercial Drive to landscape a parking spot—complete with patio furniture and books to read. The parking space lawn was put to use by local residents for the entire day.

As we proceeded, we realized how much fun we were having and how easy it had been to move from idea to action. A look around our table at meetings made it clear we were no superheroes, not especially daring or tough folks. We understood that if we could do it, anyone could. So we created 'zines to share learned tips and to try and spread the culture jam bug to others in our city. Putting the 'zines together was an extension of our creative work, and leaving them around offices or cafes, or wherever else we went, became part of our jamming.

During our active years in both cities, we communicated some important messages. We may have even started local debates when our actions made the news. It was certainly our hope that some people were moved by what we did, that our jams put consumer culture into perspective, encouraging further questioning. Yet we did wonder from time to time if our actions were pissing people off. To be honest, I think we were more interested in a quick comeback to the mainstream rather than a reasoned argument for change. Certainly, the snarky "you don't know shit" tone carried by a lot of our culture jammed messages wasn't designed to win the hearts of hardened conservatives.

I'm quite sure that those who participated in these collectives would agree that the greater share of the benefits from our culture jamming were claimed by the crew itself. As we executed one action after another, we began to walk taller in our cities and to take the mainstream media environment around us a lot less seriously. After all, we knew that if we really didn't like what we saw day after day, we could get together and alter it within a week. Changing the culture that produced the ads, well, that would take more time.

adbusters: culture jamming consolidated

For almost three years in my life, culture jamming was both a renegade night-time pursuit and a 9-to-5 day job. I worked with Adbusters Media Foundation, the self-designated "culture jammer headquarters." This nonprofit organization, founded by documentary filmmaker and former marketer Kalle Lasn, started in the early 1990s as a small Vancouver-based outfit, and has since grown into a kind of radical media empire.

While some activists have been trying to be heard in the mainstream for quite some time, ADBUSTERS has had the uncanny ability to insert jams into dominant culture since its inception. After creating their many "subvertizements" (print ads which mimicked mainstream brands) and "uncommercials" (subversive TV and radio spots), Adbusters Media Foundation would first present them to the middle-sized audience of their ADBUSTERS MAGAZINE and website. These subvertizements and uncommercials were often picked up and mass distributed by mainstream media, and over the net from person to person.

Working at this hub of activity and dissemination was, for me, a position of cultural privilege. Judging from outside responses, a good number of others felt empowered by this work as well. In the well-executed culture-jammed products that ADBUSTERS provided, some found a powerful written and visual language for their distaste of consumer culture. This is significant since these same people often felt that their values are misunderstood and misrepresented by the mainstream. But there have been as many who were continually signalling their disillusionment and dissatisfaction back to ADBUSTERS in letters to the editor and articles in other activist media. People often painted ADBUSTERS as a big money-maker profiting from subversion. This, I can tell you, is off the mark. No one at ADBUSTERS, at least while I was there, was making a decent salary, including Lasn and, being a non-profit organization, all profits from the magazine and fundraising are fed back into the organization.

McDisease
A O
D W

This disappointment towards ADBUSTERS may have something to do with the promises of the rhetoric found in the magazine's communications. In its dispatches, ADBUSTERS would often take the tone of a movement leader, hinting at an emerging nation of culture jammers. But was it really spearheading a cultural movement? The Media Foundation put almost all of its energy into producing and packaging subversive media products, doing the culture jamming themselves. The many that responded to ADBUSTERS' call-to-arms wanted a piece of the action but instead came away with a magazine, a poster, a website. As much as it is impossible to package experience—the active ingredient of culture jamming—it is equally impossible to consume it as a product.

what does the future hold for jamming?

Our cultures are changing more rapidly than ever before. What may seem a good idea one moment becomes yesterday's news the next. Though culture jamming has recently been on the rise, some have already written it off as an over-popular tactic that has been co-opted by the mainstream. But does the tainted image of culture jamming on the larger scale affect the way it can empower the individual who does it on the street? What possibilities does this practice hold for the near future?

It is worth asking how long culture jamming will remain an alternative form of expression. After all, flexible dominant systems, like consumer capitalism, readily co-opt subversion by taking-on the tactic themselves. Take for example Nike's practice of jamming its own soccer shoe billboards in Australia and ascribing the actions to the fictional activist group fighting for "fair play," as in "competitive advantage in sports," not "labour practices."

To address the overenthusiastic beliefs of Kalle Lasn and others who believe that culture jamming will bring about the revolution, I would offer a cautious observation. First, if this vision involves an elite troop of culture jammers bombarding a majority audience of spectators and consumers with more products and messages, then we shouldn't hold our breath. No major social change has ever come as the result of clever messaging alone. Though, in retrospect, we associate passionate slogans and iconography with major social movements. Much of the momentum behind them came from unseen political, demographic, and economic factors—these unseen forces gave rise to messages and not the other way around. However, if it's a question of larger numbers of people doing the culture jamming themselves, then I think there is potential for a significant shift. There is an undeniable transformation that takes place when people break out of their consumer roles and start to creatively talk back at their culture. Through this process, the consumer becomes the producer even if only for a moment. If more people do this, the trend towards cultural self-determination will accelerate. What results from this is anyone's guess but I'm generally in favour of autonomy spreading out as far as possible. With people able to increasingly find their voices amplified through blogs and other online media, I think we're already seeing more self-determination.

Though I'm critical of culture jamming as a means of communication, I think culture jammed products do have the power to seduce the willing into becoming future activists. Perhaps the analogy of the "gateway drug" works here: a mild narcotic that gives the user a taste for something harder, like pot smoking that leads to heroin addiction, except in this case, harder is healthier. I still remember the jolt I felt after stumbling upon my first

Adbusters Media Foundation's anti-car TV ad, placed just after a driving show on the CBC. The sense of vicarious complicity I shared with this bit of media sabotage was one of the experiences that nudged me down the road to culture jamming. Though the first creations of new culture jammers are inevitably riffs off the mainstream, many evolve to include broader tactics and civic involvement as part of their regular activities. They get involved in building sustainable lifestyles, in lobbying for mainstream political change, or attending their first protest, or becoming involved with other autonomous media. In this way, the process of culture jamming may be the first step towards sustained political action, moving the participant from critical engagement to constructive engagement.

Though culture jamming may not be a self-contained recipe for social change, as an autonomous practice, it may be the perfect accompaniment to working for change. It introduces the necessary element of play into our relationship with mainstream society and its media by providing a creative and emotional outlet—a chance to mess with established cultural mores. It helps us live more easily with our culture's idiosyncrasies. It can be an essential morale booster for those who take everything too seriously and it can help keep us going through those long dark hours of world-changing.

notes

To comment on this essay: http://www.progress.koumbit.net/?q=node/view/124

web resources

Billboard Liberation Front: www.billboardliberation.com
Culture Jammer's Encyclopedia: www.sniggle.net
Adbusters Media Foundation: www.adbusters.org
Memefest—International Festival of Radical Communication: www.memefest.org

"caution, in 200 metres, starting wednesday, august 7 : the deportation of algerians by immigration canada, 2002"

INDEPENDENT

a tool for international solidarity building

by andréa schmidt

REPORTING

"Stupid people think this area is crazy or ali baba (full of thieves) or something but when people come to the area they see that this is life. This is human, this is also human, I think." Khalid's voice is alternately musing and firm with conviction as he reflects on the world beyond the taxi we are in. Out of all the reports I did from Baghdad, this is my favourite. It is a radio interview with Khalid and Ahmed, two young men who live in Thawra, a slum on the east end of Baghdad that is home to approximately two and a half million predominantly Shiite Iraqis. The neighbourhood and the people who live there were largely isolated throughout the era of Saddam Hussein's Baath regime. During that time, Thawra's name, which is Arabic for revolution, was changed to Saddam City; the schools and hospitals were decimated; the political repression was brutal; and foreign journalists and other visitors from abroad were kept out by secret police.

During the first year of the occupation of Iraq in 2003, Thawra remained isolated by poverty and was more or less ignored by the international corporate media and by independent reporters because it was not a centre of overt military resistance to the occupation. And like poor urban areas all over the world, it was regarded with fear and disdain, even by the wealthier members of its own society. Later on in April of that year, Thawra, known by then as Sadr City, would grab the international media's attention as Moqtada Al-Sadr, a young Shiite cleric, led the Mahdi army—a militia recruited primarily from the ranks of unemployed young men from the area—in an uprising against U.S. occupation forces.

But the interview with Khalid and Ahmed was done before all that. It was really just a recording of our conversation in Ahmed's beat-up old taxi as they gave me a tour of the neighbourhood where they had grown up. They talked about the history of the area and pointed out how members of the community had organized against the chaos of ongoing poverty and occupation. Networks of mutual aid were being coordinated through the mosques, and committees had been established to direct traffic, distribute food, and form militias to defend the neighbourhood. During our ride, they explained the names and histories of different ayatollahs (the highest-ranking and most learned Shiite religious authorities) and sayyeds (descendents of the Prophet Mohamed) honoured in ubiquitous posters. They speculated about why everyone said it was too dangerous to go to Sadr City. They spoke of their own longing for justice and for freedom and of their hopes and fears for their occupied and brutalized country.

I had left Montréal for occupied Iraq a month and a half earlier, arriving in February 2004, almost a year after the U.S./U.K. invasion. During the three months I spent living in Baghdad as a delegate of a Montréal-area solidarity project, I wrote a series of reports about daily life under occupation that were distributed through email networks and re-posted to various websites. I also produced an almost-weekly radio segment for CKUT 90.3 FM's Community News Collective. As darkness fell that evening in Thawra and we drove on to the sounds of Muharram music playing in the streets, I imagined Khalid and Ahmed's words transforming familiar Montréal apartments on the radio waves of CKUT 90.3 FM, calling the inhabitants of each room to mobilize and act for the justice these two young men wished to see.

Activists like myself land in places like Iraq, Palestine, Chiapas with big aspirations. We arrive wanting to stand in solidarity with peoples resisting occupation and struggling for self-determination. Often, we come from the very North American and European countries that are perpetrating and supporting their oppression and impoverishment. And frequently, we have only a limited knowledge of the history of the regions or the peoples we seek to support, a precarious grasp of the local language, and organizing skills developed in the streets (or universities) of cities like Montréal, New York, or London. We show up carrying digital cameras, mini-disc recorders, cell phones, video cameras, and laptops—the tools of independent reporters—and a conviction that these are also the tools of solidarity.

At best, different forms of activist media can be used to foster international solidarity with people and movements struggling to resist forms of occupation, genocide, and economic exploitation. Independent reporting, blogging, photography, radio reporting, and audio and video documentary-making can be ways of projecting the voices of those people who are on the front-lines of the struggles and who live each day with the consequences. Their voices, efforts, and aspirations are rarely acknowledged, let alone amplified, by international media reports. Our goal as solidarity activists and independent reporters is to present a radical challenge to a global order that is fundamentally unjust. It is a global order shaped by the practices of Western states, whose elites deploy military invasions and establish asymmetrical trade relationships in countries and communities around the world to facilitate the siphoning of natural resources and the exploitation of people. To be truly subversive of this order, activist reporters must go beyond simply streaming these front-line voices back to North America and to Europe.

The twenty-minute radio piece that developed out of my conversation with Khalid and Ahmed is a good starting point for reflecting on the task of building international solidarity through independent reporting. I like to think that piece achieved some of the most important aims of independent reporting used for that purpose. To begin, it amplified the voices of two young Iraqi men who are not part of the political or economic elite and who therefore do not have access to international media or to an audience of activist and progressive radio listeners in North America. It offered those listeners a glimpse of Thawra and occupied Iraq as the much-loved home of two young men with hopes and aspirations for themselves, for their neighbourhood, and for their country. In so doing, it undermined the portrayal of Thawra by international media, the occupation authorities, and the former Iraqi elite as a no-go place characterized by brutality and criminality. The report also destabilized the international media's silent claim that the only parts of Iraq that are important enough to report on are those where there are battles between occupation forces and armed Iraqi resistance fighters.

Activist reporting as an autonomous media practice does not simply offer the possibility of subverting the dominant narratives and portrayals established by the corporate media about what is going on in places of struggle around the world. In projecting the words and voices from those who are seldom heard, explaining the significance, the costs, and the hopes of their struggles, media activists seek to catalyze active and effective solidarity movements in their countries of origin. Given the ways in which global power and privilege operate, these are frequently the very countries which are directly perpetrating or indirectly supporting the occupations, genocides, and economic pillage in the places to which we travel and from which we report. This makes the prospect of contributing to the development of solidarity movements that are effective inside the belly of the beast—within the well-defended borders of Western nation-states, and close to their centres of political and economic power—vital to this form of activist media.

This contribution can take many forms, depending on the characteristics of the movements it is meant to support, their locations, and their activities. For example, in Palestine, another occupied land, members of the International Solidarity Movement (ISM) routinely send out email reports describing the day-to-day forms of humiliation and violence survived by Palestinians in prisons, at checkpoints, on the street after curfew, and in their homes. The emails of ISMers also give accounts of demonstrations, direct actions, and other acts of resistance to the occupation in which they have participated alongside Palestinians. These email reports are easy to mass distribute and to copy and reproduce in flyers, 'zines, and newspapers. By writing and disseminating these email reports, ISMers seek to contribute to the awareness-raising efforts of Palestine solidarity organizations in Western countries, as they campaign to persuade financial institutions to divest from Israel or demand that their governments take a stand at the United Nations against Israel's violations of international law and apartheid policies.

Reports written by media activists in Iraq have focused on the destruction of Iraqi neighbourhoods by occupation forces' tanks and rockets, or on families' experiences of house raids and detention by the military. Like the ISM reports from Palestine, they have been a key component of North American and European anti-occupation groups' campaigning efforts to demand that state governments and corporations collaborating and profiting from the occupation withdraw their support. Anti-war and anti-occupation groups have reproduced and circulated interviews with Iraqis who are living the reality of military violence and economic theft by U.S./U.K. military forces and corporations on websites, blogs, and email lists. They have tried to use the reports of media activists to re-focus public attention on those who are most affected by the occupation but most frequently eliminated from media reports and occupiers' calculated statements. The way in which North American media keep careful track of U.S. military casualties in Iraq, but are quite lax in their reporting of Iraqi deaths at the hands of occupation forces, is a basic example.

Activist reporting, as a tool of international solidarity, attempts to link local and global struggles, trying to build a bridge between two localities that compels people in one struggle to take action that supports the desire for justice and the right to self-determination of people in another. As it forges this connection, activist reporting calls on its audience not only to be active participants in its reproduction and dissemination but also in the actions and activities of solidarity movements themselves.

the failures of activist reporting: repeating colonial patterns

The activist reporting that I observed in Iraq lived up to neither its own potential as a practice of international solidarity, nor to the principles of openness and participation promoted in the concept of autonomous media. It is worth being critical of activist reporting practices in Iraq—and in all the other places around the globe that have become international solidarity hotspots—because that critique is a way of articulating what independent reporting as an international solidarity building tool could be.

In theory, autonomous media aims to amplify the voices that are drowned-out by dominant discourses in order to critique, challenge, and ultimately transform the oppressive economic, political, and social institutions that mute those voices or make them incomprehensible. Autonomous media producers recognize that these voices are not their objects but that they belong to people with agency and with dignity. Media production becomes autonomous media production when it strives to find horizontal ways of engaging those people in media production. It tries to break down the exclusive authority of so-called expert media producers by extending

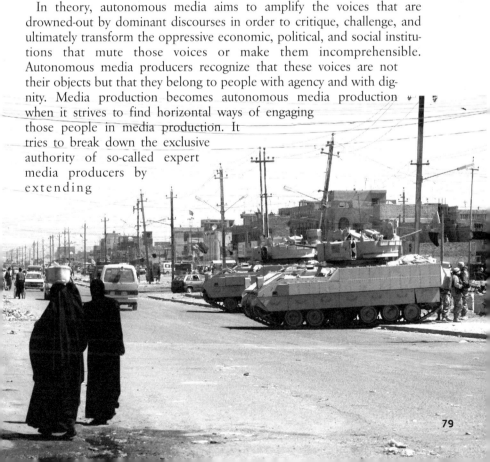

the tools and skills of media production to as many people as possible, and by drastically re-conceiving the conventional relationship between a media producer and his or her subject as a collaborative relationship of complicity between a multiplicity of potential media producers.

Far from drastically re-conceiving anything, activist and independent reporters in Iraq operated much like the corporate media teams stationed in Baghdad. True, we were not embedded within the U.S. military; we adamantly refused to be co-opted so blatantly into the occupation authority's propaganda machine. Furthermore, most of us did not stay in hotels protected by occupation forces or mercenary militias, shielded by blast walls and razor wire. We usually shunned the militarized exterior and the internal decadence of marble lobbies and turquoise pools as absurd and offensive manifestations of expatriate wealth, and stayed instead in homes, apartments, or, if necessary, in cheaper hotels. At a time when the non-Arab staff at CNN was not allowed to leave their hotel after 5 p.m., we functioned autonomously in that we told ourselves we could go wherever we needed to go, whenever we needed to go there. And when we went, we took battered taxis, not giant SUVs manned by private security.

But although our living arrangements may not have been luxurious, our solidarity reporting repeated a structure of information extraction and flow that is very much characteristic of a traditional colonialist relationship between the metropolis and the colonies. Nineteenth-century Belgian explorers travelled to the Congo to extract precious minerals they would send back to enrich their countries' coffers. English anthropologists journeyed to India to extract knowledge of the natives' behaviour to send

back to British centres of scientific learning. In the same way, independent reporters arrived in Iraq with a pre-formulated agenda—to denounce the U.S./U.K. invasion and occupation—and went about extracting the experiences, encounters, and quotes that would allow us to send convincing dispatches home.

One of the problems with this model of activist reporting, if it strives to realize the anti-authoritarian promises of autonomous media, is that the information flows only one way—from Iraq (the colonized country) to the West (the colonizing states). Autonomous media aspires to be open, horizontal, and to promote the participation of both its intended audiences and those whose voices it amplifies. It flows in many directions at once. Activist reporting from Iraq and Palestine deliberately calls its European and North American audiences to action. But seldom, if ever, did the activists sending reports from the North American and European anti-war and anti-occupation movements engage their Iraqi interlocutors in the process of media production. Seldom did we make it a priority to ask Iraqis to frame the questions to which they would respond, nor did we approach the people interviewed for their reactions to and critiques of the reports we had produced.

To the extent that it can be considered a genuine part of autonomous media, independent reporting usually draws its political vitality, creativity, and subversiveness from its accountability to social movements. For an example close to home, what makes activist reporting special, as produced by CKUT Montréal's Community News Collective, is not that CKUT's reporters and producers have perfectly honed political frameworks or direct access to some pure truth regarding the issues they cover. What makes it exceptional is the fact that the people who produce the reports are often in close relation to the movements they broadcast. CKUT listeners hear advocates of migration justice interviewing members of non-status movements, members of anti-poverty groups doing documentaries on gentrification and homelessness in the city, or survivors of the child removals system collectively creating a series on various aspects of that system.

These media producers have intimate knowledge of the politics they address, and have long-term relationships and commitments to individuals and groups within these movements. This makes both interesting and accountable reporting possible. Indeed, the people who constitute those movements are bound to hear, read, or watch the final reports. They can and do respond to them, calling the claims of the activist reporters into question or adding to them. In the process of autonomous media production, engaged audiences are also the engaged political agents who can use the reports as a jumping-off point for ongoing reflection and debate about movement principles, strategies, and/or activities.

In contrast, activist reporters from North America and from Europe tended to have poor connections to Iraqi communities, particularly those that were the most repressed, impoverished, and isolated by Saddam Hussein's regime. This is not surprising, given the history of dictatorship within the country, and of Western intervention and aggression against both the country and the region—a context into which, like it or not, activist reporters arrive as foreigners from invading nations. However, there were remarkably few concerted attempts by independent journalists to develop longer-term, sustainable relationships with those communities or neighbourhoods, let alone with emerging social movements, that would have allowed for collaborative media production or multi-directional flow of information and debate.

Building longer-term relationships, whether in Iraq or elsewhere, confronts activist journalists with a number of challenges. The first set of issues is most pressing for, and maybe even specific, to activist reporters. The other two sets of challenges are of concern to all international solidarity activists.

First, there are the issues of time and productivity. As activist journalists, we take pride in our ability to work quickly to meet deadlines and to move unfalteringly to secure the interviews, meetings, and stories that we want to produce. Those are the trademark skills and qualities that define us. Both journalists and activists feel pressure to hit the ground running, to get organized, and to produce reports as soon as we arrive in a given place. Waiting two or three days for good contacts is frustrating; the notion of living in and getting to know the people and social terrain of one neighbourhood for a year before producing a single report is almost unimaginable. The pressure to produce reports rapidly is compounded by the fact that activist reporters are frequently funded by movement organizations expecting to see the immediate results of their financial support. For independent reporters witnessing the daily violence and profound injustice of occupation, corporate colonialism, and genocide in regions around the world, the pressure to produce is also heightened by a legitimate sense of moral urgency to do something.

Secondly, to build relationships, particularly relationships that lead to greater solidarity, activist reporters, and solidarity activists in general, need to know what groups they want to build those relationships with. And those groups must be organized enough to be able to determine their relationship with foreign solidarity activists—organized enough to invite us to work alongside them or produce media with them, and ready to ask us to leave when we are no longer useful. If indigenous groups and organizations of this sort are not inviting us to be there as activist journalists, or if we cannot hear or identify those groups, then our journalistic skills cannot be used to build truly horizontal forms of international solidarity. In these circumstances, our journalism can't really fulfill the transformative goals of autonomous media. This is not to argue, however, that we cannot do perfectly respectable conventional journalism, but activist journalism in the service of international solidarity building and conventional journalism are two distinct projects.[1]

Finally, the process of building long-term political relationships in conflict zones is an inherently complicated one. It may well involve negotiating relationships with a range of political parties, organizations, or social movements that make competing claims to be speaking for the people. This is a particularly fraught question in places like Iraq, in which the American occupiers—like Saddam's Baathist dictatorship and the British colonizers before them—exploit the religious, ethnic, and political differences to mitigate popular resistance to their oppression using divide and conquer strategies. Moreover, it is slow work to build political or personal trust in places crawling with informants and secret service and in which communities facing brutal state and military repression have developed a justified skepticism of people arriving from outside.

These dilemmas and challenges are significant. While the uneasy relationship between the desire to produce reports, on the one hand, and the need to do the slow work necessary to build accountable and long-term relationships, on the other, might never be perfectly resolved, it is clear

that the failure to prioritize the development of long-term relationships undermines the potential of autonomous media for solidarity building.

In the context of occupied Iraq, the consequences of that failure were particularly glaring. While I was there I observed that it effectively limited independent reporters to making interventions that followed the same schedule and pattern as the international corporate media. We chased the same bombs and explosions, and reported on current events as they were announced from the Coalition Provisional Authority's press theatre in the Green Zone—though it is possible that our vantage point in the Red Zone lent a different flavour to our reports. We relied on the same translators and fixers to set up meetings and to interpret for us during interviews.

Consequently, we tended to frame our reports with the same stifling and impossible-to-answer question as the corporate media. The question that was surreptitiously posed to any Iraqi who met a Western reporter during the first year of occupation: "Was life worse before the invasion, or after—under Saddam, or under the Americans?" The result was relatively superficial, one-tone reporting, in and of itself worthy of condemnation. But all the more deserving of criticism is the method of media production that gave rise to the question—or failed to give rise to better ones. Activist journalists seeking to build the sort of solidarity that can undermine and transform global systems of domination that powerful transnational elites are committed to maintaining should never be content to ask people living and struggling under a brutal military occupation whether one brand of fascism is better or worse than another. The fact that we couldn't come up with better questions to ask suggests that we hadn't built the sort of trusting and respectful relationships that would have allowed us to frame questions able to give expression to Iraqi aspirations—their aspirations for so much more than what exists under occupation or what had existed under Saddam's regime. I don't think it is a stretch to believe that the same collaborative relationships that could have provoked us to ask anti-fascist questions would prove to be a strong basis for international solidarity and to be sustainable even when the violence and devastation of the occupation stops headlining the news.

harnessing the transformative potential of autonomous media

It is not impossible to imagine a different practice of independent reporting that would genuinely live up to the anti-authoritarian promises of the autonomous media movement that has engaged activists around the world. Such a practice would both rely on and help to foster relationships, discussions, and debates between individual solidarity media activists, as well as the broader movements that support them and rely on them for information.

Independent reporting within an autonomous media context would involve a willingness on the part of activist reporters to put aside the deadlines imposed by our daily blog entries and international mass-mobilizations. It would require that we slowly build long-term relationships with individuals, communities, and movements—relationships that privilege a multi-directional flow of information and voices and that require independent reporters to be accountable to the communities featured in their reports.

In this model, each report could be used as an opportunity to strengthen the relationship. A report would be viewed as an opportunity for collaboration with people, not just as an opportunity to ask questions. Completed, it could and should be shared with the people who were interviewed or an even broader group from the community or movements to which they belong. Our

collaborators could then evaluate it, tell us if we have misinterpreted or misused their words and ideas, and engage in debates with us, and with each other, on the political perspective we have brought to our reporting. A report might then be able to function as a catalyst for coordinated international actions within the framework of a solidarity campaign. Or, it might instead illuminate points of political divergence and proximity between our political positions as individuals, between the movements to which we belong, and between the positions internal to those movements.

This practice of activist reporting in the service of international solidarity presupposes that we are wanted and welcomed by a given community or social movement, whether in Iraq or elsewhere. It is very possible that there are times and places in which international solidarity building through activist reporting is not possible because no movement has called on activist journalists to collaborate with them and so no long-term and accountable political relationships can genuinely be developed. I would argue, in retrospect, that such was the case in Iraq. This conclusion points less to the limitations of activist journalism as a tool of international solidarity than to the need for serious reflection about the necessary preconditions for any sort of meaningful solidarity work at all.

Being transparent about our reporting practices and using reporting as an opportunity for collaboration and dialogue could strengthen the capacity of this tool for building international solidarity movements. The strength of relationships built through such a model of independent reporting will be matched by the capacity of activist journalists to bear witness to the dynamics of resistance to occupation, neoliberal exploitation, and genocide carried out across the globe. In a parallel sense, those who practice this type of activist journalism will be more accountable to the communities for which they seek to mobilize solidarity abroad. This practice of collaborative and accountable activist reporting will harness more of the subversive and transformative potential of autonomous media in the interest of building strong, dynamic, and honest international solidarity movements.

"a year of occupation"

notes

[1] While it may seem obvious, it is important to articulate the caveat that activist media projects and independent reporting undertaken as a tool for international solidarity are not the same as indigenous, locally-driven media projects. They do not perform the same functions, serve the same audiences, or open up the same spaces for dialogue, action, or resistance. In Iraq, for example, after the invasion and in the first weeks of occupation, dozens of new newspapers sprang up in Baghdad. Radio Dijla (Tigris Radio)–an Iraqi version of AM talk radio–was launched in the spring of 2004 and provides a forum for Iraqis to speak out about the issues that affect them on a day-to-day basis: lack of security, electricity failure, and the occupiers' empty promises of reconstruction. These Iraqi-driven media initiatives project the voices of Iraqis to other Iraqis, and to the Arab world more broadly, allowing for a range of exchange, political debate and rhetorical and active forms of resistance within Iraq that independent reporting, no matter how collaborative and accountable, never can.

web resources

Andréa's reports from Occupied Iraq: www.en-camino.org/iraqreports
CKUT 90.3 FM: www.ckut.ca
International Solidarity Movement: www.palsolidarity.org
Iraq Solidarity Project (Montréal): psi@riseup.net
Radio Dijla: www.radiodijla.com

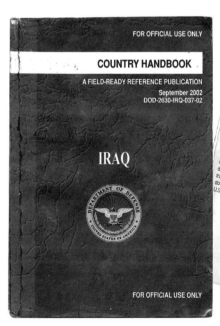
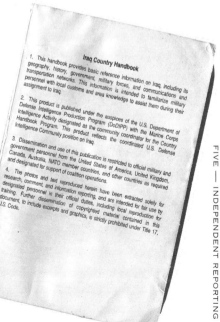

ECHOES FROM

street newspapers and empowerment

THE CURB
by isabelle mailloux-béïque

> "you really can't have true democracy
> until there's equal access
> to all means of communication"
> — Steven Dunnifer[1]

where it all began...

Street newspapers play an important role in processes of social change. By refusing to be silenced, the voices of street journalists challenge dominant discourses and put forward dissenting views on social realities. Montréal's street newspaper, *L'ITINÉRAIRE*, serves as an excellent case study through which to examine the importance that street newspapers play in marginalized communities.

First, it would be fitting to describe myself a little, because the stories to be told here are about people, ordinary people who, for many different reasons, end up in extraordinary and often extreme situations. I am such a person. I have experienced harsh alienation most of my life. I have walked a path of my choosing and was a slave to a rather dark part of myself for more than ten years. When I reached the age of 22, I realized that my self-destructive behaviour would soon lead me to death unless something drastic happened. With little faith or courage in sight, I began a provocative and drawn-out process of profound transformation. My outlook on life and on myself took a new turn.

My personal journey parallels how media activism came into my life. I realized that things weren't right, that they had to change, and that I had to be part of this change. While reintegrating myself into society—mainly by going back to university in communication studies—I once again felt alienation all around me, but this time I wasn't causing it. It was present, all around, like a heavy load on my shoulders, something I could not ignore. I was profoundly disturbed by the world we live in, with its mass-consumption, culture of performance, lies, profit, waste, violence, stereotyping, injustice, and the destruction and conformity it entails for us all.

jumping into the solution: activism

My first step towards a solution took place in the winter of 2001, during the Summit of the Americas in Québec City. Convinced that my feeling of powerlessness and frustration had to stop, I made a small but decisive move. I walked into a café on St-Laurent Boulevard to attend, somewhat nervously, my first local Indymedia meeting (CMAQ - *Centre des médias alternatifs du Québec*).

Since then, being involved in this media project has been a concrete way to follow and act upon the principles I believe in and try to live by. More importantly, I play an active role in the global justice movement. This empowering experience has led me to believe that all of us, together and in our own different ways, can contribute to imagining and putting into place new ways of being and doing.

Empowerment is at the core of autonomous media. It is a process of becoming aware of the ability to affect change. It involves freedom from oppression, servitude, and prejudice by becoming an active member in the development of individual and collective well-being. It results in a new-found sense of autonomy and power. The realization of possessing the power to instigate change may sound insignificant, but it is in fact everything.

Open and participatory in nature, autonomous media create opportunities for people to bring about change through different strategies. I have been able to witness the relationship between participatory media and empowerment in Montréal's street newspaper, L'ITINÉRAIRE. You may have seen one of its many street vendors walking through Montréal, selling the latest issue of this monthly publication. I have interviewed some of the street journalists, as they are known, that work with L'ITINÉRAIRE. It has been a rich, colourful, and insightful experience, as this chapter will reveal.

street newspapers: an eclectic movement

L'ITINÉRAIRE is not a unique phenomenon. Brussels, Buenos Aires, Cape Town, London, Montevideo, Namibia, Stockholm, Stuttgart, and Vancouver are but some cities, among many, with their own street paper. These types of newspapers, having diversity and autonomy as their strength, come in countless shapes and forms; yet for simplicity-sake, this chapter will describe the two most prominent models—the European and the American.

Regardless of the model followed, most street newspapers operate under one basic principle–they are non-profit organizations and profits must be re-invested in one way or another into services for the homeless and for poor communities. The European model usually focuses on creating economic opportunities for street vendors (homeless or low-income people). The aim is to attract readers by producing a media that will cover subjects with a broad audience appeal. Take, for example, THE BIG ISSUE, which was created in London in 1991 and is one of the oldest street papers. It is produced by professionals, and sold by street vendors facing a variety of problems. The profits of the weekly magazine are reinvested in a wide-range of services for the homeless and the socially marginalized– including health care, education, and housing–in order to help build self-esteem and dignity. This model usually overlooks both the restricted access of marginalized groups to the means of communication, and the need to democratize media.

The American model views street newspapers as far more than a way for homeless people to earn money. Media are seen as political and social tools to be used by marginalized people to gain power in society by claiming a space to be heard. Street people themselves participate in the making of the newspapers by contributing articles and stories. Seattle's REAL CHANGE has been a pioneer. The central mandate of this by-weekly publication is to give a voice to low-income people. REAL CHANGE provides writing workshops twice a week to encourage people to write and publish in the paper. Actively engaged in the fight to end homelessness and poverty, REAL CHANGE is engaged in popular education on the realities of the homeless, in an attempt to break stereotypes popularly held by society. L'ITINÉRAIRE, Montréal's street newspaper, is closer to the American model since fifty percent of its content must be produced by homeless or low-income people.

Although each street newspaper is unique, networking has proven to be crucial. Using media and communication in the fight against poverty can be a daunting task. Hence the need arises to join together, forge links, share experiences, and foster cooperation. These objectives are at the heart of the world's two main street newspaper associations, the International Street Newspapers Association (INSP) and the North American Newspaper Association (NASNA). Both work as decentralized umbrella organizations, aimed at creating common spaces and ties between street newspapers, and helping members accomplish their mission, whether by providing logistical support, political pressure, or facilitating exchanges in services.

Both INSP and NASNA identify poverty as a global problem, making their solidarity central to the battle they wage against poverty. THE BIG ISSUE, through INSP, recently participated in establishing a street paper in Japan, where poverty and homelessness have only recently been acknowledged as a social problem by the Japanese government. Encouraged by the positive public response received so far, the Japanese team hopes the street paper will help change people's attitudes toward poverty, which is often seen as a personal problem rather than as a social issue. As a way of promoting new projects, the two associations have also worked together to create a useful and practical guide on how to start a street newspaper.

montréal's underground voices

Back to the Montréal pavement where, in 1990, a group of homeless people became interested in floating a community space—somewhere off the street, somewhere they could sit and socialize together. With the help of social workers from the Préfontaine Community Centre, they managed to open a space in downtown Montréal that same year.

The community was responsible for the space and the idea of creating a newsletter gradually came about as a way of informing the homeless community about their new space. L'ITINÉRAIRE was born. The first issue came out in May 1992, put together by four people from the homeless community with the help of a professional journalist and two social workers. It included poems, drawings, and stories. Some 1,000 copies were distributed throughout community centres, clinics, rehab centres, and shelters. Three more issues were published, but interest and energies gradually waned in late 1993, and the project came to an end.

In 1994, John Bird, a former homeless person and founder of London's street paper THE BIG ISSUE, visited L'ITINÉRAIRE and shared his experiences. To Bird, the survival of street newspapers depends on two things—reaching a wide public and being active in the marketplace. This was a turning point for those interested in resurrecting L'ITINÉRAIRE. Instead of following the model advocated by Bird, they decided to hold onto the idea of a community-based newspaper with empowerment at its core, produced by a team of homeless and low-income people, as well as professionals, and to be sold in the streets to the general public. In May 1994, 10,000 copies of a revamped L'ITINÉRAIRE were sold for one dollar each in the streets of Montréal.

Today, between 18,000 and 22,000 copies of L'ITINÉRAIRE are sold by more than 100 street vendors every month, with an estimated readership of 50,000. Assisted by the chief editor and her assistant, street journalists submit articles and stories on a monthly basis. L'ITINÉRAIRE provides a unique avenue of expression for marginalized voices and ideas. It gives the public an alternative source of information because it features original content on economic, political, and cultural issues. Within the pages of L'ITINÉRAIRE, readers learn about issues silenced or ignored by the mainstream media—issues involving the social exclusion of various marginalized groups, such as sex workers, the homeless, people who receive social assistance, people living with HIV/AIDS, and those dealing with mental illness and addictions.

The street newspaper is run by the L'ITINÉRAIRE Community Group, which is headed by a board composed mainly of people from the street—people experiencing realities such as homelessness, addiction, alcoholism, and mental illnesses. The community group also runs *Le Café sur la rue* (The Café in the Street), and a space for low-cost internet access, thus offering a cohesive environment committed to the needs of the community. To sustain the different sections of the project, the Community Group employs professionals and low-income people enrolled in government programs that support community groups and workplace re-integration.

the power to exist

Listening to stories of street journalists and street vendors involved in a participatory media project can help in the examination of how resistance and empowerment are inherent to autonomous media. The power of L'ITINÉRAIRE is manifested by the opportunity for people normally excluded—not just from the media but from society at large—to speak and be heard on political and social issues. L'ITINÉRAIRE challenges the status quo by giving a voice to marginalized people thus bringing broader perspectives and alternative views to the public's attention.

It may seem strange that people find they need to create their own media in order to have a say in the public arena. But this is the reality, a reality that has been increasingly exposed by activists who argue that the current mass-media system is elitist, closed to dissenting voices, and hardly open to ordinary people and their concerns. For 54-year-old Arthur, who joined L'ITINÉRAIRE recently in an urgent need to make ends meet, it's an obvious truth. "In the mainstream press," he says, "you have to search a whole lot to find something that will talk to you socially; I mean that takes a real social point of view and defends it."[2]

Ordinary people are the ones who experience the repercussions of events reported on and discussed in the media. They concretely feel the fallout of Premier Jean Charest's attempts to reengineer the state and the recent re-election of President Bush. As a daily observer of one of the most gentrified areas in Montréal, Sophia—a L'ITINÉRAIRE street vendor who has chosen to sell her copies on a street corner in Montréal's plateau district—believes the mainstream media better get real and start listening to the people affected by government policies. Linking this to the importance of street newspapers, she says, "L'ITINÉRAIRE is different from other types of media, because it talks about the real issues of people living in the streets. It's not about statistics, rumours. It's raw; it's real; it's as it is; it's current; it's what's going on."

Describing the harm caused by mass-media distortions, Nick Couldry, a British academic, speaks of the symbolic power of media in "constructing reality."[3] Access to media is highly controlled and restricted, giving an exclusive minority of institutionalized and legitimized professionals the power to define reality and to disseminate their definition widely among the general population. Gaston, one of the original contributors to L'ITINÉRAIRE, now writes chronicles in the newspaper. He's 50-something, has been off all drugs for more than 20 years, and has had a roaming life, living in the streets from time to time. He has a clear sense of Couldry's theory about the immense power of this privileged minority, and says, "Experts have a lot of power these days; they pretend to hold absolute truth." He describes L'ITINÉRAIRE as a place for truth, a place where street experience is valued as a crucial element of information. "L'ITINÉRAIRE is much more about truth, because it's people from the inside of things who write in the paper. If the paper deals with prostitution, there's likely to be a prostitute who writes an article. And who knows better than him or her about that? You won't be seeing that at LA PRESSE,"[4] Gaston says.

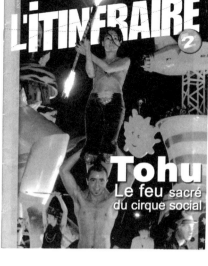

Many street journalists interviewed argue that people with experiences from the margins of society are important social experts. They may not have learned about complex social phenomena and acquired theoretical frameworks through schooling, but their life stories are definitely about core social truths. Arthur, a recent contributor to the paper, is encouraged by the attention readers give to street journalists, and says, "The vendor's tribune is really popular and that's really cool because it's the expression of people who aren't experts. It's lived experience. It's life expertise."[5] Whether for sex work, incarceration, homelessness, mental illness, or poverty, the voices of people who share their lived experiences are understood by those who work on the street newspaper as necessary contributions to the construction of social reality.

By stepping into public debate through the production of media, street journalists assert their existence. This inherent link between existence and voice is well described by Brazilian educationist Paulo Freire: "To exist, humanly, is to name the world, to change it. [...] Human beings are not built in silence but in words, in work, in action, and reflection on their action."[6] Being acknowledged and recognized is a victory in itself for marginalized people and stigmatized groups. As Robert Beaupré wrote in the pages of L'ITINÉRAIRE, "surviving traumas can produce deep wounds, making it a lifelong struggle for some to find their place in the world."[7] Gaston's reality reflects this statement; he suffered hardships in his childhood and has been fighting his inner demons for years. At L'ITINÉRAIRE he finally feels he belongs. It is where he has been able to see himself as a key figure in social change. "Step up—you have to step up for yourself in society. When you say that's enough, that's enough. You can't always be the victim of others; you have to do things to bring about change. And you don't necessarily do it to feel good, but it does feel good," he says of his experience as a street journalist.

Despite the evident power imbalance in naming, framing, and ordering social realities, the authority of mass-media to report on what goes on has become naturalized and is perceived as a given. Luckily, some people fight against this tyranny over meaning. Street journalists refuse the pervasive and highly questionable sense of normality in social discourses. Relying on their particular experiences, they negotiate what's generally considered normal and abnormal in society today by telling their stories. They also question the legitimacy of the social authorities in assessing and reinforcing social norms. Andrea Langlois, in her work on media and social movements, observes how mainstream media coverage of activism demonstrates how transgressions or alternative meanings are overlooked, twisted, and recuperated by mainstream media.[8] In its position of marginality, L'ITINÉRAIRE seeks to challenge this status quo by pushing these discourses into spaces for debate in society.

Furthermore, by making first-hand actors essential speakers of the social realities within L'ITINÉRAIRE's pages they, themselves, know too well, their voices are deservedly given legitimacy and authority. L'ITINÉRAIRE resists the mass media's monopoly over the construction of social reality by creating an opening in the public sphere for homeless and low-income people to be heard. "It's an extraordinary mode of transmission for people from the street to integrate themselves, find a job, come off of the streets, and deliver their message," says Sophia, who joined the newspaper to escape isolation. L'ITINÉRAIRE gives people the power to define themselves and to tell their own stories which isn't possible in the mainstream media. Their shared experiences work to free both the individual behind a story and the story's reader, from different forms of oppression.

From its inception, L'ITINÉRAIRE has served another more practical purpose—providing additional income to street vendors and an alternative to begging. The feminist movement has fought for women's financial independence to be recognized as a crucial factor toward emancipation. In a way, street newspapers fight the same battle. They give homeless and low-income people opportunities to attain financial autonomy. For Arthur, the inspiration to write in and sell the newspaper was based on an urgent financial need. As he puts it, "With a welfare cheque of 500 dollars a month, you can't eat for the whole month, so I'm happy to be financially independent. I can make ten to twenty dollars a day to eat, buy tobacco and a beer, and be able to function. I don't have to tax my mother; she's poor anyways."

Street vendors occupy visible social spaces, on main streets within the city, thereby making the paper accessible and necessarily linked to the social actors who have produced it—it comes out of a person's hand, not off a shelf. The act of selling the newspaper becomes part of the challenge to the stigmatization and exclusion faced by the marginalized. Stigmatization and exclusion come in many different forms; whether subtle or blatant, they linger and persist. The homeless, addicts, sex workers, prisoners, people on welfare, street kids are often regarded as outcasts in today's society. They are considered undesirable because they are thought to be unproductive according to society's increasingly persistent obsession with profitability and efficiency. It is a harmful perception for people on the margins. As Karen, one of the street vendors, says, "People have prejudices and I suffer from discrimination. I'm sometimes confronted with difficult encounters when I sell L'ITINÉRAIRE because people refuse to accept us as we are."

Despite occasional prejudices, selling the newspaper brings visibility to street vendors and attracts, in most cases, positive attention. "I have this lady who buys the newspaper every month. She says I'm her favourite journalist. It makes me feel good. I want to keep doing it," says Arthur. Street vendors engage in constructive and rewarding exchanges with passers-by. They see themselves as important players in the street, mainly because of their ability to listen and share with strangers. In the words of those I interviewed, they act as street-corner therapists, social contacts (especially for the elderly), direct sources of knowledge about different problems, and links to appropriate resources. A sense of strength arises when selling the newspaper, strength that comes out of a positive shift in public perception that reflects back onto the perception street vendors have of themselves.

Standing tall and proud while selling the newspaper on street corners, L'ITINÉRAIRE vendors work at the ground level of social change. Power dynamics may be unequal, but they insist on imposing their presence and carrying their message as front-line producers of change. Challenging people's comfort levels and indifference, vendors continue to fight the battle for public recognition of their work. "It's rewarding for me to work at L'ITINÉRAIRE. Work is the word," Arthur says. Sophia has the same take on the subject as Arthur. She does not understand what people mean when they ask her why she does not work a real job. "It's weird," she says, "when they see the delivery guy from LA PRESSE, do they ask him this question?" The sense of freedom associated with being your own boss and working your own schedule is crucial for most vendors and journalists. It is a choice they make, as valid as any other says Mike, one of oldest street vendors, "I've been doing it for ten years. It's hard, but I like to be in the street, to feel the pulse of the city. For me it's a unique way of interacting with different kinds of people." Street journalists and vendors challenge today's traditional definitions of what it means to work and to be productive, defying once again what is commonly understood as normal.

As more than a space for bringing little-known realities to public attention, L'ITINÉRAIRE is a space for what academic Nancy Fraser calls subaltern politics. For Fraser, these spaces are "where members of subordinated groups invent and circulate counter discourses to formulate opposing interpretations of their identities and interests."[9] Not only do street journalists challenge the prevalent sterility and complaisance of mainstream discourses, but through their contributions to the newspaper, they can also reclaim and create their own identity.

limitations and future prospects

In the debate around autonomous media, some would argue that L'ITINÉRAIRE is not an autonomous media, primarily because its funding comes from government programs and publicity, and that it therefore adheres to the principles of mass-media, operating under various mechanisms of control and oppression. But it can equally be argued that L'ITINÉRAIRE is not defined by where its funding comes from because, unlike corporate media, it remains a non-profit project with original content that defies dominant social discourses. The paper is very much an autonomous medium in that it is participatory and inclusive and thus offers marginalized people and groups a means for self-expression. It is a space of empowerment that is conducive to learning and experimenting.

And it is a space for the voices of resistance—a resistance that is becoming increasingly global. The voices in L'ITINÉRAIRE can be linked to larger social movements, although these links need to be strengthened. Many activists in global social justice movements seem to overlook street newspapers, although it is unclear as to why. Are such publications discredited, ignored, or simply forgotten? It is hard to say, but what is clear is that it is a challenge for street papers to be fully incorporated within a movement to which they actively contribute. An important step in the coming years will be for street papers to look beyond their own networks and to begin building bridges with the global justice movement, with the hope that it will be open to the integration of street papers and produce a wider perspective for social change.

Unfortunately, L'ITINÉRAIRE faces limitations that are common in the milieu. Most autonomous media must deal with an array of challenges. L'ITINÉRAIRE's survival is constantly at risk as the paper struggles with funding, independence, and credibility, all while trying to fulfill its mission to recruit and train new street journalists, and to appeal to a wider readership.

At L'ITINÉRAIRE, the socially accepted norms of the workplace—such as hierarchies, performance and productivity—are negotiated on a daily basis. The relationship between the production staff and the journalists is a collaboration based on the principles of respect and equality, in a common effort to make things work to the benefit of all. The staff has no choice but to adapt to the abilities and the pace of the street journalists. Although the staff is responsible for meeting deadlines and coordinating production, one of their main tasks is to assist street journalists through the process of writing. This creates tension, which has proven to be the beauty of the project as well as its foremost challenge. Some say it feels like a miracle renewing itself each month.

L'ITINÉRAIRE's most original characteristic is the population it aims to serve. Maintaining participation requires tremendous amounts of resources, energy, and time to stimulate and encourage. The balance between empowerment and economic factors is a primary concern. On the one hand, amateurism can be fatal because the street newspaper's survival depends on public support to be economically viable. On the other hand, focusing solely on quality and public response can easily lead to the sacrifice of empowerment by over-focusing on efficiency and professionalism. The tricky balance struck, which is negotiated and put to the test daily at L'ITINÉRAIRE, is its main measurement of success.

Over the years many challenges have threatened the newspaper's existence. A few years ago, because of financial difficulties, L'ITINÉRAIRE was on the verge of closing its doors. According to Arthur, the more than 100 people involved with the project would have lost a reason to live. With a sense of urgency, the newspaper went under many changes and miraculously succeeded in preventing the worst.

It now feels like L'ITINÉRAIRE is back on track. Two young professionals work together with street journalists and new collaborators to create a revamped paper with an original aesthetic and fresh content. The current team is dedicated to making L'ITINÉRAIRE attractive and interesting to its readers. The team readily admits that the main challenge is to keep empowerment as a priority. Writing for the newspaper is demanding for the street journalists and the street vendors. Many have difficulty writing or reading, and feel alienated by technology, while others still deal with addiction or struggle with mental illness. The road to autonomy can be rocky, which makes L'ITINÉRAIRE a rich, yet complex and vulnerable, media project.

last words

Active, daring, and at the forefront, street journalists play a crucial role in social change by making themselves visible in a positive and creative way. They speak up and engage in public dialogue, both through the paper and in the streets. Sophia says, "people come see me and say they read the newspaper, that they learned something and better understand certain issues. That's what gives me the guts to keep going." Well aware of its social duty to challenge insidious prejudices, L'ITINÉRAIRE persists in its mission. "It's our mission to break the prejudices people have, but it happens slowly," says Mike, who has been selling for ten years.

L'ITINÉRAIRE is a tool for educating the general public about the realities of the marginalized living in streets. It confronts pre-conceived notions and challenges widely accepted certainties. By being media producers and front-line distributors, street journalists reclaim their identities, engage in dissent, and engage in social change where it counts—right on the street corner.

notes

* I would like to express my gratitude to the gang at *L'Itinéraire* for their generosity and shinning colours. Thank you to Audrey and Jérôme for opening the doors of the paper to me. A big thanks to the street journalists and vendors of *L'Itinéraire* who generously accepted to answer my numerous questions. Finally, thank you to all at *L'Itinéraire* for adding your grains of salt to the Montréal landscape for over ten years. You do this loyal reader so much good.

[1] Dunnifer, Steven. (n.d.). Proverb. Published online at: http://www.lalutta.org/ivi.shtml [accessed March 28, 2005].

[2] All interviews with the participants in the *L'Itinéraire* project come from interviews conducted between July and September 2004 within the framework of the author's forthcoming Master's thesis (Université de Montréal). Names have been changed to maintain the anonymity of the participants.

[3] Couldry's work focuses mostly on media power and alternative media. See: Couldry, Nick. (2000). *The Place of Media Power*. London, U.K.: Routledge; or, Couldry, Nick. (2002). "Mediation and Alternative Media, or Relocating the Center of Media and Communication Studies," *Media International Australia Culture and Policy*, No. 103, pgs. 24-31.

[4] *La Presse* is the French-language agenda-setting corporate daily newspaper in Québec.

[5] The vendor's tribune is a space dedicated to street journalist and street vendors where in few words and a free style, contributors share theirs thoughts, hopes, struggles, gratitude, poems, and even recipes. It is one of the most widely read sections in *L'Itinéraire*.

[6] Freire, Paulo. (1983). *Pédagogie des opprimés; suivi de conscientisation et révolution*. Paris: La Découverte, pg. 72. Free translation: *Exister humainement c'est dire le monde, c'est le modifier (...) Ce n'est pas dans le silence que les hommes se réalisent, mais dans la parole, dans le travail, dans l'action réflexion.*

[7] Robert Beaupré. *L'Itinéraire*. No. 114, February 2004, pg. 27.

[8] Langlois, Andrea M. (2004). *Mediating Transgressions: The Global Justice Movement and Canadian News Media*. Unpublished Master's thesis: Concordia University.

[9] Fraser, Nancy. (1992). "Rethinking the Public Sphere: A Contribution to the Critique of Actually Existing Democracy," *Habermas and the Public Sphere*. Craig Calhoun (ed.). Cambridge, MA, U.S.: MIT Press.

web resources

Big Issue, The: www.bigissue.com
International Street Newspaper Association: www.street-papers.com
L'Itinéraire: www.itineraire.ca
North American Street Newspaper Association: www.nasna.org

SCREENING THE REVOLUTION

> [...]
> There will be no pictures of pigs shooting down
> brothers in the instant replay.
> [...]
> The revolution will not be right back after a message
> about a white tornado, white lightning, or white people.
> [...]
> The revolution will not be televised, will not be televised,
> will not be televised, will not be televised.
> The revolution will be no re-run brothers;
> The revolution will be live.
> — Gil Scott-Heron[1]

what is a video activist and why is that different from being a non-activist videographer?

It's important to begin by defining "activist," which can mean someone who opposes inequities in the world, in his/her community, and who works actively towards a more just society. A video activist is incredulous by nature and is concerned with the popularization of alternate truths that encourage social justice by getting visual information about an issue to an audience beyond the people directly involved. In contrast, a videographer who does not consider herself an activist may make films that do not necessarily advocate for social justice. Social change is not the primary purpose of her work. This separation is not necessary clear, as non-activist videos—whether as documentaries or as works of fiction—can also have a strong impact on the viewer and promote introspection about social issues.

People who characterize themselves as activists are engaged in activism every day. Their activism is not limited to public demonstrations of dissent. Activism is highly political but it is also inherently social and is inescapably linked to the personal. Social justice is central for the video activist, influencing decisions, relationships, topics of conversation, and the direction of their videos. A self-proclaimed video activist looks through a camera's lens as influenced by her approach to activism. The camera becomes a tool of choice for social change, much like the megaphone, litigation, a can of spray paint, a website, and/or poetry may be among the tools of choice for others.

Another important factor that may define a video activist is her relationship with a community of activists. Videographers with reputations as activists are regularly invited by organizers to film non-publicized actions, often receiving little information before the action other than where to meet. Within an action or demonstration, a video activist's role is to document the event with images. The resulting footage can be used by campaign organizers to advance an agenda through the creation of promotional or educational videos. It is equally useful as a debriefing and self-criticism tool for activists seeking to determine the relative success of a campaign or action. For those arrested, the footage can potentially help them formulate a legal defence. It may also help in the identification of police infiltrators masquerading as protesters—caught on-the-fly making an arrest. The images can also provide important historical documentation of a changing society from the perspective of those who are actively attempting to change it, and by providing an alternative to the status quo perspectives most often shown on television.

Despite all the potential uses of a video activist's footage of demonstrations, it cannot be overstated that video activists are not limited to filming demonstrations or interviewing protesters. Any issue can be the topic of an activist's video because mass convergences do not monopolize organized denunciations of an established order. Highly subjective references and deeply personal experiences can equally challenge the policies and perspectives of the status quo. Images of a neighbour being forced into the streets by an inability to pay speculative rent increases, scenes of large swaths of deforested land, or an anecdote of a racist exchange can also denounce unjust situations. A video may deliberately omit status quo points of view because they are sufficiently represented in mainstream media. This subjectivity may also distinguish video activism from traditional documentary journalism, which pretends to be what doesn't exist: objective. Video activists do not fane objectivity, but proudly engage in presenting opinions—marginalized or otherwise—aimed at inspiring public debate and encouraging action to instigate change.

Video activism reaches beyond video making. It also delves into the process of organizing by forming collective structures to assist in the production and distribution of activist videos. Based in Montréal, the *Collectif de vidéastes engagéEs Les Lucioles* (Les Lucioles Video Activist Collective) is one such example. It was formed in the spring of 2002 to provide video footage for *Le centre des médias alternatifs du Québec* (CMAQ - Québec Indymedia), but altered its mandate during its first meeting to produce video for distribution anywhere. Four months after its founding, the collective hosted the first public screening of its works, which quickly evolved into a quasi-monthly event with a consistently-packed house. At each screening, the collective invites an alternative media group to present their medium to the audience in an attempt to promote alternative information and encourage the habit of seeking out multiple sources of information. During intermission, the event becomes a democratic platform, when Les Lucioles offers an amplified soapbox to community organizers with news and announcements to share and the screenings have become convergence spaces for many local and regional activists. Three years into the project, Les Lucioles show videos from other local, regional, and international videographers and have developed an extensive archive of nearly 20 VHS & DVD compilations of each of their premiere screenings.

The strength of such a collective is the diversity in content and form of their videos; a diversity that is unique to autonomous media. Take for example Santiago Bertolino's 2003 video QU'EST-CE QUE L'OMC...[2] (WHAT IS THE WTO...?). In this film, we see footage–recorded by three Les Lucioles members–of the mass arrests during the mini-ministerial WTO meetings and protests in Montréal. Their cameras were recording from both outside

"with surveillance comes repression. resist."

and inside the police barricades, as observers of the arrest and among those arrested, respectively. The footage from within the encirclement of riot police, as they sealed off the entire street, was unique because mainstream television cameras recorded only from the outside at a safe distance, as mandated by police.

Just as different activists have diverse priorities, video activists have different approaches to their films. One such example is Joachim Luppens' 2003 stop motion animation, ASPHYXIE ALIMENTAIRE[2] (FOOD ASPHYXIATION), which has vegetables escaping from their Styrofoam and cellophane prison only to return after witnessing the murder of other escaped cellmates by knife wielding hands. VOL SOCIALEMENT ACCEPTABLE[2] (SOCIALLY ACCEPTABLE THEFT), by Julien Boisvert and Stéphane Lahoud, follows a student through a supermarket who steals expensive food for a Christmas dinner she is hosting for her mother and her mother's girlfriend. This 2003 work of fiction plays poverty versus profits during a season with intense societal pressure for mass consumption. The short video L'INCONSCIENCE[2] (UNCONSCIOUSNESS), submitted anonymously to Les Lucioles, portrays a hidden character brushing her teeth in full view of a running tap with the sound of teeth brushing in the background. The viewer is forced to watch as the water pours down the drain for the entire brushing. This short video, which links personal hygiene to water conservation, has the potential of entering a viewer's personal space every time he/she brushes his/her teeth and may debatably have greater impact on the viewer than the same issue treated in documentary style.

at large protests like the summit of the americas in québec city in 2001, there were hundreds of video cameras recording all aspects of the mass convergence. what has made video such a prolific tool for activists, and why are so many people now using video?

Activists are not the only ones carrying video cameras these days. The police have also discovered the utility, accessibility, and malleability of video.

Surveillance cameras blink at us from in front of television monitors and behind secure walls. They film protesters as a means of intimidation, to gather evidence against them, and to develop their own database of activist portraits for face-recognition technology like they did in the London Borough of Newham on October 14, 1998.³ Add to this the number of cameras carried by activists themselves, and the answer is yes, there are a lot more cameras at demonstrations these days. The accessibility and relative affordability of video technology—the cameras for capturing images, the computer and software for processing the images, and the DVD burners, video projectors, and websites used to screen and show the videos—have made potential filmmakers out of anyone with the inclination.

Most people know someone with a video camera used for weddings, birthdays, holidays. There are interesting issues or stories that need to be recorded and retold that are not necessarily about celebration. The latent video camera that is sitting in a friend's or a sibling's closet is just begging to be used. Like all technology, as it ages, it becomes cheaper, which may explain why video is increasingly used to communicate dissent.

Video hasn't always been as prevalent as it is today. Nam June Paik was among the first to film with a portable video camera when—in 1965 from inside a taxi—he filmed Pope Paul VI parading through New York City. He later screened his footage in Greenwich Village. Video had the perfect formula to attract growing numbers of videographers: a video camera's portability made it possible for a one-person film crew. And in addition to its manageable size, video cameras were much cheaper than their film predecessors. The images could be instantly played after being recorded without further processing and video cassettes could be reused.

If AMERICA'S FUNNIEST HOME VIDEOS marked the death of the home video with its television premiere in 1990, then George Holliday introduced video activism to the mainstream on March 5, 1991, with video footage he took from his apartment balcony in South Central Los Angeles. He captured, and had broadcast, police officers beating Rodney King. There were Scott-Heron's images of "pigs shooting down brothers"[1] replaying over and over again on prime-time television. Holliday's 81 seconds of footage helped transform the personal video camera from an accessory for nostalgia into an effective, prevalent tool for social justice reclamation and human rights advocacy. Visual proof is very influential—viewers

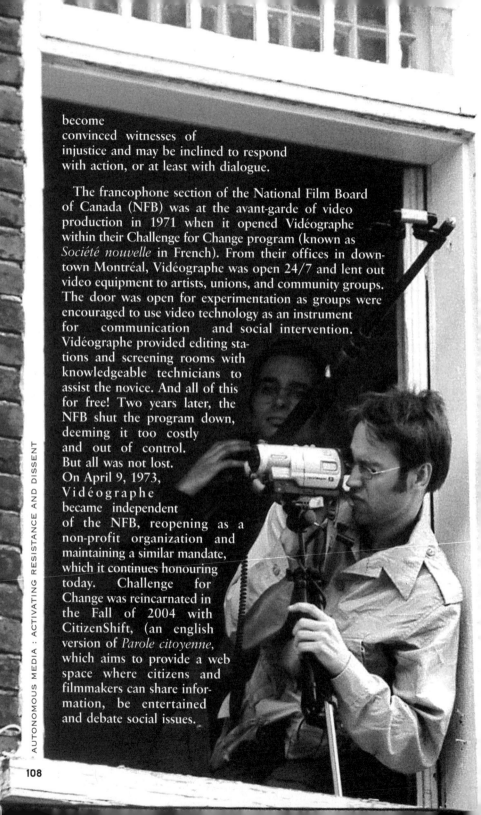

become convinced witnesses of injustice and may be inclined to respond with action, or at least with dialogue.

The francophone section of the National Film Board of Canada (NFB) was at the avant-garde of video production in 1971 when it opened Vidéographe within their Challenge for Change program (known as *Société nouvelle* in French). From their offices in downtown Montréal, Vidéographe was open 24/7 and lent out video equipment to artists, unions, and community groups. The door was open for experimentation as groups were encouraged to use video technology as an instrument for communication and social intervention. Vidéographe provided editing stations and screening rooms with knowledgeable technicians to assist the novice. And all of this for free! Two years later, the NFB shut the program down, deeming it too costly and out of control. But all was not lost. On April 9, 1973, Vidéographe became independent of the NFB, reopening as a non-profit organization and maintaining a similar mandate, which it continues honouring today. Challenge for Change was reincarnated in the Fall of 2004 with CitizenShift, (an english version of *Parole citoyenne*, which aims to provide a web space where citizens and filmmakers can share information, be entertained and debate social issues.

the discreet filming of rodney king's beating shows that human rights abuses may be more prevalent when violators feel as though they are untouchable because of their status within an established power structure. is the medium of video good at preventing human rights abuses?

George Holliday's videotaped images—as interpreted by Witness, an international organization that uses video and technology to fight for human rights—gave the beatings impact with an urgency that words alone are unable to provide. His footage did not prevent the incident but was used in a trial against the police officers who assaulted King, which didn't really help the case, considering the acquittal of the police. However, Witness claims to prevent human rights abuses with the use of video cameras.

Witness empowers grassroots movements by providing them with computers, imaging and editing software, satellite phones, and email. The organization provides training to use all of this equipment to communities in distress. This allows them to collect images, which are regularly included in official human rights reports governments give to the United Nations, to counter information presented by the same government officials who commit the human rights abuses. Communities using video equipment can develop a self-protecting voice with their footage but only after the images have been seen by others or included in official reports. There are times when human rights abuses have been prevented by the presence of rolling cameras, which shield the abused with potential visual evidence against the perpetrators who are reluctant to continue abusive behaviour when witnesses are present. And a camera can have the effect of impersonating a witness or group of witnesses. Public opinion can be swayed to support vulnerable people and their communities against oppressive measures by the state, by corporations, and others.

The cameras Witness provides can link local and international communities. Compromising footage gets screened and campaigns develop in support of the abused, beyond the immediate area where the abuse is taking place. But the relationship between the local community and the international presence can be particularly precarious. An international observer with a camera may more easily deter abuse in their presence than a local using the same camera, therefore alternate strategies are needed to empower people—whoever they are—behind the camera. For example, since it's more risky for the human rights abuser to implicate foreigners than it is to further abuse the locals, international observers may want to flaunt their cameras, openly promoting the fact that they are filming, while locals may need to be more discreet.

This prevention strategy has been successful for Witness and those they support. The Witness-type strategy has also been successful for groups like *Projet Accompagnement Québec-Guatemala* (Québec-Guatemala Accompaniment Project), the International Solidarity Movement, *Comité chrétien pour les droits humains en Amérique latine* (Christian Committee for Human Rights in Latin America), the Iraq Solidarity Project, and others who send international observers on-location with vulnerable communities to prevent abuse with their presence. Cameras can have the same effect—even after international representatives have gone—but only if that footage has an escape route to an audience that is prepared to popularize the abuses and take action to prevent their repetition. So, cameras can prevent abuse, but it seems only after initial abuse has begun.

is there collaboration on videos that address issues that straddle international boundaries other than acting as witnesses for prevention purposes?

When filming an issue in one place, a videographer could easily include images from a related issue somewhere else in the world: the treatment of homelessness in Montréal versus a refugee crisis in Darfour, inexpensive goods in local stores and sweatshops in Mexico, or resource extraction by an Alberta corporation in Colombia and human rights abuses near their oil wells. Communication between media activists from different continents is as diverse as the issues they follow. Just as capitalism crosses borders to increase profits for those with the most capital, collectivism promotes global collaboration among video activists who share raw footage, exchange and translate films, and often work as a group on a single film whose topic is not limited to a single location.

Practitioners of video activism are as transnational as the corporations they denounce in their films. When a fight for access to water in one hemisphere is linked with a struggle for shelter in another—with convincing images to back up both claims—video activism thrives. As interaction among activists from different backgrounds, continents, and ethnicities expands, established colonial relationships between the haves and the have-nots have the potential to crumble with irrelevance. So instead of privilege imposing an assistance model of interaction, where aid, knowledge, technology, and expertise flows downward to those labelled as "under-developed," a model of collaboration is used whereby assistance is horizontal and of multilateral benefit. A videographer from Saskatoon shouldn't need to go to Chiapas, Mexico, to capture successes of the indigenous struggle to accentuate his video about native self-determination in Saskatchewan. Networks are developing that could allow an unfettered exchange of images for both community's benefit. Copyleft[4] is de rigueur in video activist circles where information exchange and solidarity outrank capitalist tendencies of ownership.

Big Noise Tactical Media is a "collective of media-makers [from] around the world" who base their collaborations on the plurality of their unified voices. Their 76-minute film, THE FOURTH WORLD WAR (2003), was produced by "a global network of independent media and activist groups" in a common effort to oppose war. They create media as an anti-capitalist tactic that has them embedded within resistance movements in provisional collaborations. Big Noise makes a distinction between temporary and permanent structures of resistance. A permanent willingness to develop alliances—and a temporary, malleable capacity for actual collaborations on projects—is their tactic to avoid being criminalized by capitalism's hold on systems of justice. As projects begin and end, different collaborators enter and leave the common effort with a fluidity that defies detection. Such a collaborative effort created the film KILOMETER 0 – THE WTO IN CANCÚN (2003) about protests against the WTO in Mexico, which was an Indymedia co-production with Mexico's *Acción Informativa en Resistencia* (Informative Action in Resistance), Big Noise Tactical Media, Promedios, Denver Revolution, and *Calle y Media* (Street and Media).

Another example of a transnational alliance was initiated by Angad Bhalla's 2003 film UTKAL GO BACK. The footage of a community in active struggle against global mining interests was taken while visiting Kashipur, India. After showing the film in Montréal, local activists initiated a campaign directly pressuring project shareholder—Alcan—where it is headquartered. Alcan't in India is a transnational campaign acting on multiple fronts, displaying that collaboration is the nutrition for the collective's appetite, both within a collective and among them.

"no to the free trade area of the americas."

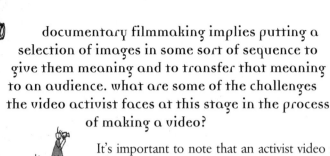

documentary filmmaking implies putting a selection of images in some sort of sequence to give them meaning and to transfer that meaning to an audience. what are some of the challenges the video activist faces at this stage in the process of making a video?

It's important to note that an activist video is not by definition a documentary film that tries to capture a slice of reality by following real people through real events. Like those described earlier, there exists a wide range of activist video styles and genres. There are fiction, animation, mock news casts, music-style video clips, sampling, and other genres that effectively impact the audience with a unique approach to an issue or cause. The downfall of video activism would be to stick to the predictable genre of following protesters through a snake march, then capturing the arrests toward the end. This is necessary but it's only a sliver of the potential.

Whatever genre of video the activist chooses, there are indeed challenges in putting it together. One of the bigger challenges during the production of a video is the editing phase because too few people have access to editing stations with powerful enough computers to handle the editing software and the massive file sizes. Even fewer people have ever used editing software.

Video neophytes regularly approach recognized video activists to ask for assistance on a film with footage that has been sitting in a drawer. Before really getting into video, some activists didn't know what to do with all the high-8 or mini-DV cassettes that were accumulating in boxes under their beds. They watched unedited footage by connecting their cameras to a TV or VCR. Video editing capabilities have only recently developed into powerful, affordable software created for the home-based personal computer rather than solely for commercial film production. Take a few zeros off the price, include most industry standard features, and more people will buy it and share it with friends.

Besides the technological challenges, choosing which footage to keep and which to discard is highly subjective, and since the recording is often improvised at unscripted events, the editor may be left with hours of footage with divergent themes and mixed qualities to choose from. There is occasional pressure from the main actors in a filmed event or action to take the video in a certain direction in line with a campaign strategy or to get the video out quickly to promote the cause at an upcoming scheduled event. Depending on the level of collaboration between videographer and actor, this added pressure can help or hinder the editing process and the quality of the final film.

It is because of these challenging factors that many video activists have organized themselves as collectives to share experience, equipment, tactics, footage, editorial input, and film credits during the production of a video. Two members may film an event, another may film subsequent interviews, while a fourth may digitize and edit the footage, and another may translate and prepare subtitles, then another may export the final film on a DVD and design its cover, while yet another may organize a screening event. The collective organizational structure is common among media activists who share the burden of equipment ownership, and the benefit of expertise.

short of taking formal courses in video production and post-production, how have video activists democratized the production of videos to produce the high quality films we are getting used to seeing?

On any one website or at any single night of screenings there is a gamut of film quality. And quality does not refer to the subject or to the approach, but rather to the comprehensibility of the subject, to the camera skills in the footage, to the sound quality of the recordings, to the footage selection made by the editor, and to the effects and transitions of those images in the final film. One of the challenges for the media activist, whether in audio, text, or video, is to develop a pool of creators who are familiar with the technology, have access to it, and are prepared to put in the time needed to develop a story and follow it through to a conclusion.

A quick scan of activist organizing will show a lot of activity going on within a collective structure, where the members take the time to discuss issues, make decisions by consensus, share skills and responsibilities, and take collective credit for their successes. It is within this structure that skills are most often transferred from one activist videographer to another. The mentor-apprentice relationship is often informal and the teaching/learning that takes place is bi- or multi-lateral. When a common objective binds the collective to a series of shared tasks, both learning and teaching embellish the landscape. When a collective collaborates with others in a coalition, skills are shared beyond the initial group.

There have also been considerable efforts to formally teach videography skills to others. Vidéographe is still actively training people in the community to use video equipment, although they no longer do so for free. Other recent initiatives have introduced marginalized people to video and trained them with skills to produce their own independent videos. In November 2001, *Télé sans frontières* (TV Without Borders) was initiated to provide training to young people—with space reserved for street or marginalized youth—to learn to produce their own videos, which are later screened on the organization's website and on Télé-Québec, the provincial public television station.

The francophone section of the National Film Board continues to play a role in the development of independent filmmakers. In June 2004, it supported the brainchild of filmmaker Manon Barbeau, who sought to provide a creative outlet for indigenous youth in Québec via an itinerant production suite called the Wapikoni Mobile (Wapmobile). The 34-foot RV had enough space to receive 12 creative producers at once and included the latest equipment to film, edit, and screen the finished videos produced by native youth from the Atikamekw and Algonquin Nations. The Wapmobile returned to Montréal in November of that year and transformed itself into *Vidéo Paradiso* for several weeks. It was parked in Square Viger (a popular hangout for homeless youth) to offer video training for any street youth interested in taking the challenge. They later drove to Québec City to repeat the process. By December, *Vidéo Paradiso* had an 81-minute compilation of video shorts. Wapmobile's federally-funded equipment was passed on again in collaboration with *Dans La Rue* (In The Street)—a street youth support centre—by lending its equipment to support an integration program where homeless youth are guided through a steep learning curve of expression through video.

Montréal seems to be a hotbed of video activity but it is certainly not the only place where videographers are sharing their skills. In Chicago, Street Level Youth Media is a non-profit organization that puts the latest video technology into the hands of urban youth to produce a quarterly

30-minute interactive TV program. The show, called LIFEWIRE, airs on a Chicago public access cable TV and involves about one thousand youth per year in Street Level's programs, which go beyond video training.

In addition to these, and other, training programs, one can find activist handbooks and 'zines developed by video activist collectives to initiate the beginner.[5]

An important media-related issue is access—access for independent media producers to broadcasting, print, or screening opportunities, and access for media consumers to independently-produced information. what's the use of making videos if no one will be able to see them?

Taking footage with a video camera is relatively easy. Editing the footage is somewhat more difficult because of the technology issues mentioned earlier. Screening or broadcasting to an audience adds new challenges to the equation. The absence of permanent distribution venues—whether on TV, at movie theatres, or in film rental outlets—has forced activists to improvise with a diversity of tactics for getting their videos to an audience. The most prolific spaces for viewing the work of video activists is certainly the internet, either directly from video collective websites, from Indymedia sites that invite autonomous submissions of videos, or from other sites that promote video production and include activist films in their repertoire. Too many sites (even activist ones) force potential viewers to buy their films, without the option of viewing them online or downloading them for free. This may be due to video's large file size and space limitations on the servers used to host their websites. It may also be explained by a historical and cultural bias within capitalist systems that is difficult to shed, where one is expected to (at least) recuperate one's costs. Other reasons include fundraising efforts to subsidize court costs for activists arrested within the context of a video, for financing further video productions, or to help acquire equipment to continue the practice. This is understandable but if video activists are concerned with the popularization of alternate truths, efforts must be made to get the videos seen by as many viewers as possible. If free distribution is required to reach a particular audience, then free access should be provided.

Video networks have developed on the web as distribution hubs for activist videos, which are sold, downloaded, and viewed online. The Video Activist Network is probably the most popular site to view and buy videos from activists around the world. The website includes links to other videographers and activists, and how-to manuals. Indymedia's NEWSREAL is another source for prolific web distribution, as is its cousin, EUROPEAN NEWSREAL. Other than internet streaming, creative initiatives and collaborations have emerged to get independent/alternative video images to a receptive audience.

The Toronto Video Activist Collective (TVAC), which has been around since 1999 to, in their words, "shamelessly promote social and environmental justice issues through the production and distribution of activist videos."[6] They sporadically hold screenings and distribute VIDEO ACTIVE compilations in select retailers in Toronto. TVAC has distributed its work in collaboration with Satan McNuggit Popular Arts (SMPA), which was established to "actively support initiatives to [...] replace corporate and statist models of media production."[7] SMPA may be found at alternative book, 'zine, and music fairs where they sell their wares directly to the public.

Le Rézo, a network of alternative screening venues (in cabarets, bars, cafés) throughout Québec, was created to bypass corporate theatre chains' inaccessibility to independent film productions. They screen a rotating selection of films, scheduled months ahead of time and promoted via internet networks and through supporters living in the areas where screenings are held.

Les Lucioles have developed a modest distribution network of supporters that extends beyond those who attend their regular screenings. They established a subscription program with college groups, student unions, teachers, and NGOs, by accepting donations in exchange for a selection of their compilations. Their videos are also screened at fundraising parties, conferences, festivals, and ad-hoc events, often organized by people with a stake in one of their films.

The growing popularity and number of issues-inspired videos being produced and needing audiences, will only encourage more initiatives to get dissenting images to people who want to see them, to those who don't, and, more importantly, against the wishes of those who would prefer the images to stay out of sight. Based on the volume of activist videos being made by a diversity of producers, on the high quality of their productions, and on the popularity of screenings, there is reason to be optimistic.

has television become the vaulted bastion of the corporate elite or is there room in for independent, even dissenting, voices on tv?

Community television seems to be in an uphill battle in Canada. In 1997, the Canadian Radio-Television and Telecommunications Commission (CRTC) devised Bill PN 1997-25, effectively allowing cable companies to provide public access TV channels at the cable company's discretion and on their own terms. According to Star Ray TV, a community television station that has been trying to get a low-power broadcast license since 1999, "the result of this policy has led to much frustration for local and independent producers who seek public access to their local 'community channel.' Today the vast majority of cable companies use these channels as little more than promotional vehicles to sell their other services, and are anything but accessible to the general public."[8] As cable companies centralize their production facilities, they close community production studios, effectively removing the community from the production.

A more recent CRTC notice (2002-61) officially recognizes the autonomous community TV station model, which exists, for the moment, only in Québec. The notice guarantees a minimum of 30% public access programming—produced by community stations and broadcast by cable distributors—making it virtually impossible for cable distributors to ignore content provided by community stations located within their network.

The Canadian Broadcasting Corporation (CBC), as a public broadcaster representing the national community, should also open its studios to a percentage of content, produced by people who are not staffed by the broadcaster, but who come from the community as volunteers or are otherwise paid by the broadcaster for content provided. CBC producers have, in the past, disallowed video activists to provide their own images to represent themselves—to avoid biased reporting. This is probably more representative of a producer's tactic for self-preservation, rather than an attempt to maintain broadcasting integrity. As the ratio of advertising increases on CBC television, it seems unlikely that alternative, confrontational content will increase with it, although a program like ZEDTV, which invites autonomous submissions via the web, have introduced a breach in CBC's methods for acquiring content. This breach needs to be ripped open to allow dissenting voices to take a greater portion of the public airwaves

what do you see on the horizon for video as a source of autonomous media? is the activist video, like the home video, already dead?

What lies ahead for video production will follow what has already happened with print publishing. Small press publishing has become an important source for some very unique and high quality literature that is taken seriously by authors and readers. The books coming from small publishers are often better-designed, unique objects that are increasingly supported by independent booksellers.

When desktop publishing became the norm, anyone with a computer and the typesetting software could publish a book and print as many copies as a budget could afford. Video production has reached the desktop, and now it's taking off. So expect a lot more video productions, more unique ways of showing them to an audience, and more support from indy video retailers whose customers will increasingly ask for independent/alternative productions. And with activism and dissent on the rise, expect to see increasing numbers of activist videos on neighbourhood walls, on café screens, and on festival schedules. Just as innumerable photocopied 'zines are flogged and traded, now-standard DVD burners are multiplying copies of activist videos for easy hand-to-hand distribution.

But are there enough video (media) activists out there? The debate continues as to whether too much information will drown the consumer. Information, disinformation, misinformation, propaganda, and all other forms of knowledge transfer should not be discouraged. Audiences need to develop instincts to seek out many sources of information—not just what they agree with—from all types of media, not simply the medium that gets to them first. Media activists who create information and pass it along to others, need to promote the multiplicity of sources to their audiences and to others who passively receive information from monolithic corporate spindoctors masquerading as news providers.

The revolution—in whichever form it assumes—is indeed being screened. Unedited footage is being shared by producers who have only met through email. Collaborative projects are ongoing between community workers, social justice promoters, media activists, and event organizers, creating networks that make it easier for videographers to film, edit, and screen their works. As the proliferation of information from community groups around the world is more easily shared and accessed, divergent struggles are being linked. Perspectives within activist videos are widening, even when local issues are the focus, making them more interesting and more relevant in a globalized world. More videos are being seen by larger audiences who expand their knowledge base to better defend and debate issues of concern. Permanent production and viewing alternatives are enduring in full support of the ad-hoc initiatives that preceded them.

If video activists continue to experiment with video, the medium, as a tool for dissenting voices, will survive. As long as the growing global community of social-equity advocates persist with the struggle for justice, and video activists capture and share their enthusiasm, the medium will prosper. This is the future of video activism.

notes

[1] These lyrics are excerpted from the introduction "The Revolution Will Not be Televised," in Scott-Heron, Gil. (1970). *Small Talk at 125th & Lenox*. New York: World Publishing.

[2] These are videos that were either produced by Les Lucioles or were shown during their premiere screenings and included on one of their compilations.

[3] Newham, England has 140 CCTV cameras and 11 mobile radio units that disregard the Data Protection Act. These cameras capture images for the Mandrake Face Recognition System. The information was taken at: http://www.spy.org.uk. More about British video surveillance (with aprox 1.5 million recording cameras, a 1 camera : 50 people ratio). Published online at: http://www.notbored.org/8june01.html [accessed March 23, 2005].

[4] Please see page 4 of this book for Cumulus Press' definition of copyleft as it refers to this particular volume.

[5] A few titles are: *Guerrilla Video Primer* by the Cascadia Media Collective; *Video Activist Handbook* by Undercurrents; Paper Tiger TV's *How-To Resources to Video Activists*; GNN's *How To Shoot a Guerrilla Video*; I-Contact's *Video Activist Survival Kit*; the *Human Rights Witnessing Training Manual* by Witness; and *Le petit guide pratique (The Little Practical Guide)*, by Les Lucioles.

[6] Taken from TVAC's Background History. Published online at: http://www.tvac.ca/about/history.html [accessed April 1, 2005].

[7] Taken directly from their manifesto. Published online at: http://www.satanmacnuggit.com/manifesto.htm [accessed April 1, 2005].

[8] From a press release dated, October 15, 2002, *CRTC Threatens Community TV Operator With Criminal Charges*. Published online at: http://www.srtv.on.ca/press10.html [accessed April 1, 2005].

web resources

Alcan't in India: www.saanet.org/alcant
Big Noise Tactical Media: www.bignoisefilms.com
Calle y Media collective: www.calleymedia.org
CitizenShift: citizen.nfb.ca
Denver Revolution: deproduction.org
European NewsReal: newsreal.indymedia.de
Guerrilla News Network: www.guerrillanews.com or www.gnn.tv
I-Contact: www.videonetwork.org
Indymedia Québec: www.cmaq.net
Indymedia's Newsreal: newsreal.indymedia.org
Informative Action for Resistance: kloakas.com/aire
International Solidarity Movement: www.palsolidarity.org
In the Street: www.danslarue.org
Le Rézo: www.cocagne.org/FCCV
Les Lucioles Video Activist Collective: www.leslucioles.org
National Film Board of Canada: www.nfb.ca
Paper Tiger TV: www.papertiger.org
Parole citoyenne: citoyen.onf.ca
Promedios: promedios.org
Québec Alternative Media Network: www.reseaumedia.info
Québec-Guatemala Accompaniment Project: www.paqg.org
Québec Public Interest Research Group: ssmu.mcgill.ca/qpirg
Satan McNuggit Popular Arts: www.satanmcnuggit.com
Star Ray TV: www.srtv.on.ca
Street Level Youth Media: streetlevel.iit.edu
Television Without Borders: www.telesansfrontieres.com
Toronto Video Activist Collective: www.tvac.org
Undercurrents: www.undercurrents.org
Video Activist Network: www.videoactivism.org
Vidéographe: www.videographe.qc.ca
Wapikoni Mobile: www.onf.ca/wapikonimobile
Witness: www.witness.org
Working TV: www.workingtv.com

Since 1998, a new form of communication has emerged and flourished, encouraged by the combination of internet users wishing to share information and the development of free, easy to use platforms. Wedded to self expression and existing mainly outside of the monolith of mass media, weblogs—commonly called blogs—are a new form of media whose uses are just beginning to be understood and theorized. Blogs have become important tools for activists and independent thinkers around the world, allowing for the creation of new spaces for self expression, knowledge sharing, and networking online.

A weblog is basically an online journal, a space where ideas and actions can be documented and shared without restrictions around format or major technological know-how. The new possibilities that weblogging offers as a form of autonomous media are worth considering from an activist's perspective—as space for self-publication and as a new medium for information gathering. Weblogs can be conceptualized as the ultimate form of autonomous media, whereby an individual completely controls the content of her or his own blog. However, most bloggers (or blog editors) are working complex online and offline networks, which mediate and determine, at least in part, the content of their weblog.

With the rapid development of information technology in the twentieth century, there has been a return to the idea that these technologies will benefit the masses. A few years ago, some folks started talking about blogs as the beginning of online freedom, and the term "blogging revolution" actually had currency for a while. But it is vital that in addressing the values and possibilities of blogs, we remain grounded in practice, not off in some online utopia. That said, to properly introduce the blog as a tool for activists will also require an analysis of the limits of weblogs and of their usefulness for media activism.

welcome to the blogosphere

The first weblogs began to appear in 1998, in what was then a realm confined to true techies for whom the main topic of discussion was technology and web development. Seven years later, most blogs use free platforms, which allow them to update a simple interface with text or images without having to manipulate complicated html or javascript codes. The development of this user-friendly software late in 1999 lead to an exponential growth in weblogs, and today there are an estimated three million weblogs online.

```
from:     rebeccablood.net
subject:  weblog description

message:   The weblog is at once a scrapbook, news
           filter, chapbook, newsletter, and community.¹
```

The name weblog reflects the original use of the technology—blog editors would comb the internet for sites and information that caught their attention, and then post it, keeping a sort of online logbook. The form and style of blogs changed as they became widely adopted as modes of self-publishing. Blog editors post comments or links that are of interest to them, on any topic that they please. There is no such thing as an expert blogger, people with blogs come from many subjectivities to share information online. Many blogs take the form of online journals, with links and text, however, the diversity and number of weblogs in existence today makes any generalization of what constitutes a blogger style difficult to justify.

The distinguishing feature between weblogs and websites is that a weblog is updated more frequently—often more than once a day—with the newest entries appearing at the top of the page. Weblog entries, called posts, are the main content of the blog, the idea being that if you find a weblog you like, you can check back the next day for a new post. Returning to the same site numerous times can result in an exchange of information between the blog editor and the visitor, creating links between them, and expanding blogger networks.

Another feature which was initially unique to weblogs is the easy to use comment form, where blog readers can leave their response to a post instantly and easily. Popular blogs may receive dozens of comments on each post and blog editors often use their own comment form as a method of replying to those who have left comments on a given issue. Posting comments can be an anonymous and safe venue for people who wish to have their say but are not ready to reveal their political stripes, or it can be a personalized way of asking the writer to visit your own blog.

Blog users today range from school teachers posting activities for their students to corporate media reposting their top stories in a keep-'em-coming-back weblog style. Part of the mainstream discussion around blogging is centred on the ambiguity of the word blogger, which is as open to interpretation as the word writer. Instead of getting into a debate on semantics, I would like to concentrate on conceptualizing weblogging as a participatory, autonomous media with the capacity of encouraging social change. Central to this possibility are activists; for whom weblogs can serve as tools for self-publishing, archiving, and the documentation of struggles.

a view from the inside

Since there are no rules or definitions for how to write a weblog, subjectivity is both a strength and a limitation of the medium. The majority of weblogs are personal journals and diaries that do not move beyond intimate life stories and day-to-day events. However, for activists interested in publicizing their struggles or for independent journalists posting from the field, blogs offer a space for more serious discussions. Through links to primary sources, organizations, and other media, activist bloggers can legitimize their own content at the same time as they raise awareness about other resources on the web.

Activists using weblogs to post material related to the organizations they belong to and the struggles in which they are involved are keeping a public record of their activities while at the same time archiving their thought process. The dual nature of this type of content results in unprecedented possibilities of sharing often private struggles with a larger public, and asks that our traditional ideas about who makes media be thought through again. This is particularly true because activists who do not consider themselves writers in any traditional sense, are contributing to new media production online. Furthermore, they are challenging the supremacy of mainstream media by producing their own subjective media, and are

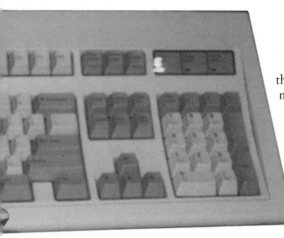

thus participating, indirectly, in the media democracy movement.

I started blogging about British Columbian politics in early 2002, a time when I was also very active with community groups and grassroots organizations in the greater Vancouver region. My weblog was useful as a tool to document and archive the sources that I was using to arm myself with knowledge against an information manipulating government. I was able to make links directly to sections in the HANSARD index (transcripts of parliamentary proceedings) or corporate annual reports to back up my arguments, and would often restyle text from my weblog and post it on Vancouver Indymedia or send it to my local newspaper.

Through cross linkages with bloggers working on political issues in British Columbia, I came to know other people in my region writing on similar issues. This virtual network allowed me to read citizen and activist perspectives on what was actually happening in B.C. politics and allowed my readers to access a young feminist's written work, which may otherwise not have been available.

Opening on the global, blogs have allowed marginalized voices to emerge online as seeds of resistance against information monopolies. The best example of this is likely that of the Baghdad blogger, known as Salam Pax, an Iraqi who updated his blog from Baghdad during the U.S. invasion that began in 2003. Writing in his blog titled WHERE IS RAED?, Salam Pax offered a subjective, on the ground view from occupied Baghdad that was missing in mainstream media. His links and writing referenced other Iraqi bloggers and information sources, allowing visitors to his blog, to access independent information coming out of Iraq.

Another fine example of an activist blog is librarian.org, where Vermont-based librarian and anti-censorship activist Jessamyn West has been posting since 1998 about issues of concern to librarians and readers in general. Explaining the content on her blog, which she updates daily with an inside view of the way libraries work in America today, she writes, "I'm not a reporter, but I like to think that I help people access the news." To this she adds, "The explosion of library weblogs and websites over the last several years makes me happy; news is less likely to fall through the cracks."[2] This comment points to the strength of weblogs from an activist's view—they provide information that is otherwise missing from the mainstream media.

In B.C.'s Okanogan Valley, activists working to start a campus radio station have been using a weblog to disseminate information about their media project to a wider public. Cameron Baughen, who's behind the weblog, explains that their "weblog allows people to quickly see what we have accomplished, keeps a history of our exploits, and means people don't have to rely exclusively on email."[3] Posting links and minutes from meetings allows the group to stay organized and to pass its link to newcomers, reporters, or other people interested in their project, bringing them up to speed on the status of the organization.

Some go so far as to argue that blogging is journalism, however the real stuff of journalism—working on the terrain, doing interviews, and using quotes—is most often missing from blogs. In the world of blogs, the burden of proof is on the writer, and in terms of ethics, Rebecca Blood has suggested six standards bloggers should strive for. These include linking to online references, posting only what you believe to be true, correcting mistakes but never deleting or rewriting any entry, noting questionable or biased sources, and disclosing any conflicts of interest.[4]

That said, a blogger is not automatically a journalist, but weblogs have been used by independent journalists as permanent or temporary spaces to publish their writing and work. The patagoniabolivia.net project is a serious but alternative independent journalism project I worked on with a colleague journalist in Latin America. We used a blog template to publish our work, included links to alternative media groups in the regions we visited, and we posted everything from researched journalistic articles to free flowing poetics and photos for our readers. The value of blogs as a tool for journalists (and especially independent/alternative journalists) is

immense, as they bring to fruition instant self-publishing accessible to a wide audience, a feat which was unthinkable ten years ago.

spinning the web

The idea of a weblogging community stems from the practice of bloggers checking other blogs and commenting on them, using a hyperlink to allow the reader to visit the blog in question. Linking between blogs is a form of networking, by which a blogger can record her or his feelings on the usefulness or accuracy of another blog or information source. It is also a way of inviting readers to check out other blogs and information sources. Each blog therefore acts not only as a storehouse for information but also as a point of connection with other blogs, and in this way organic, non-hierarchical networks of weblogs are formed.

```
from:         <Jessamyn West> librarian.net
subject:      community use for weblog
```

```
message:      I'm not a wide-eyed evangelist about it,
              but I think [weblogs] can serve a useful
              purpose for a community organization like
              the library, to communicate to people so they
              can use the organization more effectively.[5]
```

Keeping with the initial tradition of blogging, some blog editors concentrate on linking to other weblogs as priority number one, and thus aim to be a central network node based around a particular theme or region. The lefty directory is one of the few activist blog directories currently online, offering links to over 600 weblogs that, according to it, are "not part of the dominant Conservative/Libertarian blogosphere."[6] Using this type of site as a launching pad allows a curious reader to browse a wide variety of progressive weblogs and to access independent information from around the world.

Many activist collectives are currently using blog templates to publish news and information in a way that allows group maintenance of an activist news portal, a space for alternative news with an emphasis on networking between activist groups. Autonomy and Solidarity, for example, was started by a network of activist groups across Canada, whose members post news stories onto a main page on a daily basis. The Autonomy and Solidarity page functions as, to use their words, a "political network through which to explore the questions and debates that have been raised within the new anti-capitalist movements."⁷ Guests can log-on to the site, which is linked to other news sites as well as to regional groups, and leave comments for each article. Clicking on one of the featured regions results in news-feeds from activists in that region, as well as links to regional activist groups.

One of the differences between weblogs and other autonomous media like Indymedia is that with Indymedia, there is an open publishing policy that lets anyone post. How to manage open publishing has often dominated internal discussions in Indymedia, as folks dedicated to a truly open media site grapple with trolls overloading the server with comments or posting hate material. Most blogs are less open. They let guests post comments, and others, like collective blog metafilter, let people post threads (new topics) after they have registered and made a few comments, in the name of "getting a feel for the place." If someone is posting material that the editors of a weblog consider inappropriate, it is up to the editors alone to remove those postings and ban that person from publishing.

Group-edited blogs are, in some instances, kept by friends living in the same region. These blogs represent another kind of online network, where a chorus of complementary voices can converge and offer varying viewpoints. Other times, editors may not know each other and have decided to join forces in order to strengthen content and have a more regularly updated blog. Znet, one of the heavyweights in activist media today, has recently started a blog where major left/radical thinkers and journalists are given space to post writing and commentary on current events. Checking the Znet blog is one way of tapping into the thoughts and ideas of people working for change, without necessarily reading a formal article or a long essay.

millions of blogs, millions of missing voices

Despite the many positive aspects of weblogging, it is important not to forget that this is a new medium with an uncertain future and that although weblogs are tools that contribute to online media participation, they are not stand alone strategies for activism. Looking at some of the weaknesses of weblogs can help in the development of theories on what a more inclusive future for online media and activism may look like.

```
from:      <loboy> lowcolabs.com
subject:   techies only

message:   If you don't have the tech,
           you're basically not invited.⁸
```

The first and most serious weakness in regards to all forms of online media is accessibility. The online public is relatively small, and the so-called digital divide in Canada alone attests to the many barriers still standing between online media and marginalized communities. Most internet users with time to burn online updating and reading blogs are young, urban, and financially stable, resulting in what some have called an incestuous community of online media activists. To help narrow the gaps created by age, gender, language and income in internet use, technological skill sharing needs to be a parallel strategy alongside all types of online alternative media activism. Weblogs are an ideal vehicle for exchanging skills, because they are relatively simple to update and use, and they're free—at least for the moment.

Another serious limitation to alternative media proponents online is the corporatization of the internet. The recent release of the omnipresent search engine Google's shares on the stock exchange, combined with the company's purchase of Blogger, a top blogging interface, is a distressing concentration of online information and services in the hands of a corporate few. Many companies are beginning to introduce paying versions of blogging software, further restricting the number of people who will be able to blog. In their free (and ad free) form, blogs as they exist today are accessible tools for wired activists, and the end of free weblogs would mean a sharp decrease in blogs for budget writers.

The individual nature of blogs, in that they are normally updated by one person, may also be a factor dissuading activists from contributing and using this form of expression, and tending towards bigger online projects such as Indymedia. Conceptualizing blogs as functioning within a wide ring of autonomous information sources, and encouraging multiple editor projects and strong networks can reclaim collective spaces using the simple and accessible tool that is a weblog.

```
from:       <David Weinberger> hyperorg.com/blogger
subject:    community use for weblog

message:    What is the whole truth about blogging?
            There isn't one, any more than there's a
            whole truth about conversation or book
            publishing.⁹
```

A fourth limitation revolves around language. Blogs and blogging platforms are available in many languages, opening the channels of communication to the online public in many parts of the world. However the vast majority of online resources are in English, Japanese, and European languages. This adds to massive global imbalances in online participation and can create problems in initiating a truly international solidarity online. Moving towards a more multilingual online environment by encouraging activists to work on translations as part of their writing is another possibility for a more effective information network through weblogs.

Lastly, the sheer number of weblogs out there is a hindrance to the effectiveness of blogs as a medium for activists. Someone seeking out blogs for the first time will likely get stuck in a quagmire of personal blogs that have their own value, but that do not fit the description of media or political activism. This weakness reaffirms the need for stronger blogging networks and activist blog databases that facilitate a "progressive navigation" through weblogs.

looking forward, linking back

The big question is whether weblogs, when used by activists, have the potential to upset the status quo. Sharing information online and reading information written by citizens can help advance particular causes, but not without parallel action outside of the online sphere. Investing large amounts of time online, or confining one's actions to online endeavours is indeed likely to result in one's actions reinforcing dominant media and beliefs. A blog can easily be lost among a flood of others with no net benefit to society as a whole.

Yet, we cannot underestimate the social implications of a form of media that, whatever the content, represents a challenge to the corporate mass

media machine. Media democratization is about the re/claiming and re/creation of spaces within which to communicate. Blogs are changing the way information is seen, created, and consumed.

Publishing online as one part of a range of political activities can be a very effective way of raising awareness of any given cause. Macro examples of this include Indymedia coverage of anti-war demonstrations, which works both to notify people of the event, as well as to provide alternative coverage of these demonstrations, thereby creating a memory of these events, and buoying spirits. On a micro level, an activist's blog may lead someone—searching for a particular local issue—to a view point and links to other sources that are alternative to the information they receive in other media.

Strengthening the online facet of struggles for social and environmental justice means widening the base of activists that use blogs—as more activists start using weblogs to document their struggles, the possibilities for solidarity and learning across issues and across borders multiply. Working together, an effective network of activist weblogs can bring the experiences of people working for change onto the screens of many. Tighter and more comprehensive links between activist weblogs is the next step, as all the tiny cells organize into a force capable of encouraging great change.

If access to the internet can be improved, there is a distinct possibility that publishing online will have greater impact on wider communities. If social justice movements are to gain sustained, broad-based momentum over the internet, it will come as a result of hard volunteer work on behalf of many people working face-to-face in communities with grassroots activists, sharing technological skills. The accessibility of blogs creates the possibility of learning and teaching technology that allows self representation, and opens the door to moving marginalized voices into the public sphere.

notes

[1] Blood, Rebecca. "The Revolution Should Not Be Eulogised," Published online at: http://www.guardian.co.uk/online/weblogs/story/0,14024,1108306,00.html [accessed January 15, 2005].

[2] West, Jessamyn. "About librarian.net," Published online at: http://www.librarian.net/about [accessed January 15, 2005].

[3] Email interview with Cameron Baughen. March 15, 2005. Published online at: http://ouc-radio-crtc.blogsp ot.com/ [accessed January 15, 2005].

[4] Blood, Rebecca. "Weblog Ethics," Published online at: http://www.rebeccablood.net/handbook/excerpts/weblog_ethics.html [accessed January 15, 2005].

[5] Chaney, Keidra. "Catalog This: An Interview With Activist Librarian Jessamyn West," Published online at: http://www.frictionmagazine.com/politik/wave_makers/west.asp [accessed January 15, 2005].

[6] Linse, Brian. "Sunday, July 18, 2004," Published online at: http://newleftblogs.blogspot.com/ [accessed January 14, 2005].

[7] Autonomy and So. "An Introduction to Autonomy & Solidarity," Published online at: http://auto_sol.tao.ca/node/view/2 [accessed January 14, 2005].

[8] Loboy. "11.04.2004," Published online at: http://www.lowcolabs.com [accessed January 14, 2005].

[9] Weinberger, David. "Comments, February 17, 2005." Published online at: http://www.hyperorg.com/blogger/mtarchive/003704.html [accessed March 25, 2005].

web resources

Autonomy and Solidarity: auto_sol.tao.ca
Indymedia: indymedia.org
Lefty Directory: newleftblogs.blogspot.com
Librarian.net: www.librarian.net
Lowco Labs: www.lowcolabs.com
Metafilter: www.metafilter.com
Okanogan University Radio Project: ouc-radio-crtc.blogspot.com
Patagoniabolivia: www.patagoniabolivia.net
Rebecca's Pocket: www.rebeccablood.net
Where is Raed: dear_raed.blogspot.com

For more links and details on how to start you own free weblog, visit Dawn's weblog at: inkflip.net

In January of 2003, twenty women and men of different ages and backgrounds sat down together at a Montréal community centre, drank coffee, and exchanged a couple of polite words and nervous smiles. Then the meeting started. A bit chaotic at first, the discussion quickly turned to tactics. "We need to fight Québecor Media," I recorded one as saying in reference to Québec's biggest media empire. "Let's define what alternative media is so that we can act as a group," another insisted. Some shared their experiences as long-time media activists. Others simply voiced the needs of their radio station, news website, or print publication.

We later moved onto more fundamental questions such as: What unites us? What is it that we have in common? What is the course of action? The people who attended this very first encounter of what has become *Le réseau des médias alternatifs* (RMA–The Québec Alternative Media Network) were of different stripes. There were members from Indymedia Québec and Indymedia Montréal, L'ITINÉRAIRE (a street newspaper), LE MONDE (a Montréal working-class neighbourhood paper), LE COUAC (a colourful satirical monthly), three community radio stations, plus a couple of curious onlookers.

Hopes ran high that day for our new media network, which was to be based on solidarity and a common desire to distribute alternative information and news. In the two years since that first meeting, many new members have joined, coordinated projects have been launched, and exchanges between media members have flourished.

a multitude of networks

Autonomous media networks are rooted in the struggle against media monopolies. Many anti-establishment media networks exist. There are in fact as many types of networks as there are types of autonomous and alternative media. In building solidarity, some network-minded media activists have focused on ideology. Others have built platforms for advocacy. Still others constitute content-exchange networks.

The approach a network takes influences the way it is organized, its composition, and the tools its members use to advance its cause. The Grassroots Radio Coalition in the United States, for example—which brings together thirty-two radio stations—is driven by a desire to support community radio that is ideologically leftist or radically left of centre. The way the network is organized is also influenced by these values. As its website states, "there are no dues, no hierarchy, and no bylaws."[1] Since 1996, the Coalition's main tactics for maintaining cohesion have been its annual conference and its listservs for internal communication, which help to keep the loose coalition of radio activists informed. In contrast, the Pacifica network, an older and more established project, puts the emphasis on content. The Pacifica Foundation was spearheaded over 50 years ago by KPFA, Pacifica's founding station in Berkeley, California. It unites five sister radio stations and numerous affiliates. Exchanges in content are crucial, as demonstrated by the DEMOCRACY NOW program, a popular daily show composed of interviews and research from all affiliates, broadcasted across the network. Pacifica is also a respected and established listener-sponsored alternative news source. As a network, it works first and foremost to offer informed alternative viewpoints. Every station depends on the four others for its content, although the majority of programming is created by its local communities.

Deep Dish TV also makes content exchange a priority. Self-described as the "first national [grassroots] satellite network [...] linking local-access producers and programmers, independent video makers, activists, and other individuals who support the idea and reality of a progressive television network,"[2] Deep Dish TV has been around for sixteen years. This group is, technically speaking, an autonomous media network with more than 200 cable systems in the U.S. exchanging locally-produced television. The New York central office works as a point of redistribution for activist content rather than as a forum for community TV stations. Because of this, links between stations in the network tend to be weak.

In Québec, advocacy within media networks has been, historically, strong. Many traditional networks have taken very tough stances against the government. Rights and funding guarantees have been won through

advocacy, to the point where the Québec government decided in 1995 to grant 4% of its advertisement expenditures to community media; either TV, radio, or print. In this French-speaking province, the 48-member *Fédération des télévisions communautaires autonomes du Québec* (FEDETVC - Québec Federation of Autonomous Community Television) was created in 1996. Perceiving the increase in corporate control over community television services as a negative development, the members came together to advance a stronger voice for non-profit organizations, to seek more funding for small TV systems, and to create a space for experience sharing. Content exchange is almost non-existent however, since the mandates of community TV stations in Québec are limited to local programming. The FEDETVC is a good example of an advocacy-based network, with its strong ties of solidarity between autonomous stations. FEDETVC is connected with its members, involving all of them at each step in developing confrontational actions and reports to push forward their agenda.

one step away from isolation and two steps towards autonomy

Networks are important for autonomous media. Media activists involved with blogs, open-publishing sites, independent TV stations, pirate radios, and video collectives all need to network to combat isolation. Because of their subject specialization, many alternative or autonomous media have limited audiences of people who are used to consuming a certain type of alternative discourse. This leads to information ghettos, from which it is difficult to escape.

One of the current challenges for media activists is to not "preach to the converted" but to create pathways through which the ideas and discourses developed within autonomous spaces can find their way to a more diverse audience. This challenge is further complicated by the fact that media activists do not want to water-down their discourse in order to please a wider public, and they are often overprotective of their collective identity. Thinking outside a media ghetto is a challenge because the struggles involved in changing thought patterns are time-consuming, and people involved in a particular media are often focused on specific social issues rather than on the reform of media structures. This is where media activists need to position media politics as a crucial component of social politics. Media activists and groups are also often isolated from each other, divided by diverging tactics, strategies, ideology, or by competition among them.

One solution to this isolation is the creation of autonomous media networks, within which distances between groups can be lessened. Narrowing geographic and ideological divides, as well as the competitiveness that exists within communities of autonomous media must be accomplished without losing respect of differences. A coordinated solidarity between groups is fundamental for uniting media organizations with different histories, expectations, political orientations, and audiences. The creation of networks brings together media activists, opens up information ghettos, and helps information flow to a wider audience. The ultimate goal is too encourage newly found audiences to start participating within a newly discovered autonomous media project. Autonomous media practitioners must recognize that a movement in favour of networking can strengthen a collective's identity in relation to the others and promote its autonomy.

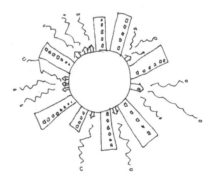

The word "networking" means, literally, working to create a net. Friendly ties between media activists or web link exchanges do not suffice, although they can contribute to the net. Campaigns and ad-hoc coalitions are other important net-type structures, although they are usually impermanent endeavours.[3] What is needed is the establishment of sustainable, flexible structures that facilitate a permanent flow of communication between otherwise isolated autonomous media sources. Well designed and well implemented networks tend to increase autonomy and reduce isolation by offering media outlets the means to prevent becoming inbred circles of activists. Networks are an important step in the creation of an ideal model of communication, in which all people can easily access, produce, and distribute information.

Networks also foster a true sense of community, creating solidarity between media organizations that are fighting similar battles, using similar survival tactics. Autonomous media networks—which can be intangible horizontal communication flows between autonomous media sources—should be formed for the benefit of all members. The idea is to avoid adding new layers of bureaucracy for activists, such as those found in more formal networks where volunteerism means additional work. Although not exactly a guarantee for survival, a network is definitely a strategy developed to preserve autonomy while encouraging sustainability.

building a network

What is a well-designed network? No single recipe exists but there are some underlying principles that can serve as a guide to network building. Autonomous media activists facing obstacles, such as a lack of volunteers or financial resources, need to determine three things before building their network. They must first identify concrete objectives. They must then define what tools are needed to attain those objectives, and, finally, they need to agree on an organizational framework.

The basic principle behind the Québec Alternative Media Network (RMA), for example, is to bring alternative and subversive news closer to the public. This self-centred objective is one that every small-scale media outlet dreams of but a network's foundation can go beyond this initial objective. The formation of solidarity and confidence among media activists is helpful for envisioning a sustainable project. All of the RMA's media lacked participants, infrastructure, resources, and money, so the service exchanges became a concrete way of expressing and practicing solidarity. This would motivate, inspire and, most evidently, help media outlets meet their mutual goals through cooperation. Networks pursuing more specific goals—such as advocacy, financial cooperation, or the promotion of its members to new communities—should acknowledge these commitments from the beginning.

When the RMA was set up, those involved in writing the founding charter had two objectives in addition to bringing alternate news closer to the general public and building inter-media solidarity. They were to document practices and support alternative media start-ups. As media activists, we are not necessarily aware of the history of alternative media in our communities. Some might be knowledgeable of an obscure Marxist-Leninist paper or community radio station in the 1970s but wider knowledge is important. There is a tendency to ignore the alternative media that existed outside urban centres, or how alternative media supported, and were supported by, social movements in earlier struggles. This ignorance—as to what media networks existed before, how they evolved, how they were organized, or why they disappeared—results in mistakes being repeated. To better understand and write about our own history and leave a trail for others to follow, documentation needs to be retained as a cornerstone of any network project.

The RMA objective of supporting alternative media start-ups, although noble, ultimately failed. Immature networks should not necessarily include the initiation of new media projects as a fundamental goal. It may add unwanted strain to assist others rather than focus on self-sustaining the members of the network.

Overall, network builders should at least consider the development of a larger audience and solidarity as good starting points and as their smallest common denominators. Objectives can be added but it's worth noting that too many can be as detrimental as too few.

media networks in practice

Following a period of discussion and agreement on major collective desires, the time comes to put a network into operation. Here, computer literacy of media activists needs to be considered, as do questions of access to technology. The challenge lies in introducing adequate technology to serve the needs defined by the objectives. For example, Deep Dish TV has satellite dishes and a budget for video cassettes and video editing equipment. The FEDETVC uses an e-mail listserv, faxes, and the like. Those who are more connected online might employ a wiki—an online text-based documentation tool—an intranet, or free software tools to ensure maximum participation and archiving at limited costs.

Technology issues may seem obvious but they are often overlooked by net-workers. In fact, many networks have lost members because of what has later been recognized as the alienation of non-technophiles. Those who do not check their email daily, or are less computer literate, tend to be marginalized from major network developments. This digital divide needs to be acknowledged and actively resolved. The choice of tools determines the culture that will develop within a network. As a knowledge-exchange forum, the Grassroots Radio Coalition values its annual conference much more than any computer-mediated tool. Face-to-face encounters remain crucial to any network design and should be balanced with and complemented by communication tools.

Along with the selection of tools come matters of process. Democracy and leadership are especially important. Should decision-making be consensus-based? Should there be a coordinating team or leaders? Most autonomous media are committed to resisting the formation of hierarchical structures, since they are often already in confrontation with vertically-structured organizations such as mainstream media and government. In his pivotal essay on alternative media and the idea of a federation of alternative media projects that he termed: "FAMAS,"[4] Michael Albert argues that the issue of organizing horizontally, even beyond autonomous ventures, is critical.

The choice of procedures and working methods vary widely, according to the nature of a network. For example, the arrival of a paid worker in an otherwise volunteer-driven atmosphere can completely shift the functioning of any network. Moreover, the organizational framework calls into consideration the crucial aspect of participation. What volunteer will sit through long hours in front of a screen, call-up other media outlets, and keep plodding once the initial excitement has faded? Participation is the mainstay on which networks rely for their survival, especially within networks built on ideals of diversity or among those insisting on building true synergy between complementary media organizations.

Participation can't be predicted but it can be valued and encouraged. Media activists need to look at themselves in the mirror. They will most likely see heavy pockets hanging under their eyes. Many media activists, patiently sitting through network meetings already put in volunteer time for their respective media, probably while working somewhere else to pay the bills. A word of advice to the tired people out there is to try and develop a rotating system in which media activists participate for a certain amount of time before passing on the torch to others. This would ensure a smoother ride for the network as well as basic accountability.

the greying institution, and the young radicals

Knowledge of how former networks functioned, such as AMECQ, along with experiences with decentralized networks, like Indymedia or the Grassroots Radio Coalition in the U.S., can help media activists uncover the many options available to them. the Québec Community Print Media Association (AMECQ) is a typical example of what can go wrong. It became a top-heavy institution, which curtailed autonomy and limited a vital component of autonomous media: creativity. Working full time in a stuffy office with others to "protect the interests of the community" is an unattractive prospect for today's network activists.

AMECQ has four staff members and forms a progressive coalition of print media. Its main goals are to search for advertisers for its members, report on the community press scene, and publish documentation of members' practices. The network has other projects, such as training workshops and conferences—with food, awards, and wine. These advantages may have appeal but its orientation and working methods resemble those of a corporate monolith. Members participate during annual conferences, while the rest of the year, the administration team decides the direction of the network. The disconnection between headquarters and its membership is too vast. This type of agenda-setting is typically the way of mainstream media.

Central to autonomous media net-working is the issue of participation. The principle of having all members participate, rather than having a centralized administration, must be pursued from the beginning.

Discussions on autonomous media networks and their ability to foster participation are bound to include Indymedia. When media activists in Seattle set up the first Independent Media Centre (IMC) in 1999, they couldn't have realized it would instigate a worldwide network of media activists. It is important to point out that Indymedia has spearheaded communication and dissemination efforts of emerging global justice movements. In the past 30 years, participants in expansive and diverse social movements have used the open-publishing platform of Indymedia

to such an extent that there are more than 100 IMCs around the world. IMCs are considered radical media by activists, essentially because of the anti-hierarchical and open ways in which they operate. Academics, like John Downing, have analyzed IMC's radicalness, as expressed in his book, RADICAL MEDIA.[5]

IMCs are interconnected through listservs. These email lists are essential to the network because they are the point of entry for every local chapter. Setting-up a new IMC requires that a local media activist collective present a proposal to the global IMC, which is then circulated on the listservs. Decisions are made, virtual meetings are held, and conflicts are resolved on the web. But Indymedia is also about offering support on the streets. Technology, money, and resource people can be allocated by the network to IMCs temporarily set-up to cover an event, direct action, or demonstration.

Among the many attractive elements of Indymedia, two are of particular importance: the handling of new technology, and the way in which the network is organized. Technologically, Indymedia can be considered avant-garde. It has incorporated open-source software to offer a platform of news publication open to the public. This includes the publication of photo, audio, text, and video content. Although IMCs are web-based, they incorporate all the media genres and formats onto a single platform. This gateway exemplifies the Indymedia ideal where anyone can rush to their keyboards to seek and produce the news. Although this has not quite materialized, Indymedia at least offers a technological tool that measures up to its utopian ideal.[6]

In terms of organization, Indymedia revives a principle of equality among participants. All IMCs in the network are autonomous and can decide to opt out of network decision-making by not contributing input to the many email discussion lists. Although Indymedia provides a framework for homogeneous practices, it gives all members an opportunity to adapt and evolve on their own terms. There is no central command centre and consensus-based decision-making is a fundamental element to all IMCs.

While this model—which promotes the concept of equality and decentralization—has been extremely successful in reawakening a wave of

media activism, it has also had its problems. New projects are sometimes dismissed simply because one person in the IMC collective doesn't feel comfortable with it. On other occasions, never-ending meetings become the norm because of paralyzing adherence to Indymedia rules on consensus-based democracy. If everyone talks for an equal amount of time—no one has more than two opportunities to speak and votes are called on every detail—everyone will leave feeling unproductive.

the RMA as a variation on the theme

In adopting a variation of the Indymedia model, The Québec Alternative Media Network's (RMA) members decided to integrate many of INDYMEDIA's trailblazing technologies—such as open source content-management systems, open publishing-like procedures, listservs and an intranet—while adapting them to their particular needs.

The idea of developing a web portal, with access to each media, was adopted right away. In one of the first meetings, some media activists were already pushing for the network to devote all its available resources, energy, and time to its creation. After collective deliberation, money was scrounged to pay a skilled media activist to build the website. Today, the RMA uses its web space as a tool for internal and external communication. It is designed to include an intranet in which a service exchange can be managed. Participating media are invited to post their needs on the electronic billboard where others can answer by putting forward an exchange proposal. RMA members wanted a multimedia experience that would have people from different types of media, providing a higher quality of services to exchange. If a photographer associated with one media could be "exchanged" for some radio air time, the network would have proven its usefulness. In addition, a reference section lists the history of emails sent.

An interactive calendar of events lists all the happenings in the network on the public side of the web portal. Syndicated news and radio streaming are accessible on the front page, as well as links to each media's website. This provides the public with a vast array of different media productions to choose from. The main advantage of having such a diversity of news in

one place is to present a plurality of voices. Even though people might not use the portal to screen the daily news, this heterogeneous space's existence is a direct challenge to the concentration of information sources, and potentially removing autonomous media projects from information ghettos. The portal also serves as an electronic archive, documenting the practices of the network.

When the portal was created, all members were aware that viewers might not identify with all of its content. News, coming from a street newspaper, feminist website, anarchist magazine, or video collective, is not all necessarily of interest to the same audience. This may be seen as an obstacle, but it is also an opportunity for each media outlet to reach new publics. The portal provided an unprecedented view of the alternative media scene in Québec.

Organizationally, the RMA chose a less formal way of making decisions. Although the founding members recognized the benefits of consensus-based democracy, as practiced by those in the Indymedia network, they knew they wanted to move away from the ideal. Every media organization would have one representative attending RMA meetings and participating in a nonconsensus-based—and rather vague—decision-making process. This passive democracy actually limited frustratingly long procedures and allowed for the emergence of natural leaders.

Although RMA members aspire to a model that gives everyone enough space to voice concerns and propose ideas, no specific anti-discrimination measures were designed. Instead, this experiment enables most involved media activists to lead the network without marginalizing other members. Leaders are designated organically as the network evolves and are encouraged to inspire less active members. The centralization of power in the hands of one particular alternative media has not happened, due to the fluid nature of volunteer involvement. Leaders come and go, which in the end balances out inequalities that could arise. The RMA therefore commits to decentralization, while accepting different levels of knowledge, skills, and contribution.

After two years of relentless effort, the RMA is now a 25-member regional network with a web portal, email lists, and an emerging service exchange platform among alternative media sources. The fact that alternative media producers had something in common, helped them to get to know one another, learn about their respective difficulties, and to overcome them through cooperation.

when the reality sinks in

Although the RMA is a success story in terms of wiring together heterogeneous grassroots media projects, it has encountered its share of limitations. One is that the web portal is not a media unto itself. Although some alternative media gain new publics via the RMA, it has become apparent that the "one-stop window" needs its own identity. It also became clear that the portal needs to be promoted outside internet-based media.

While the exchange in services is successful on a bilateral basis, much remains to be done to get media practitioners from different sectors or regions to build multilateral projects together. Since the RMA was established, a small number of new media projects have started up and others have ended. Yet, the RMA remains a symbol and a strong motivator that can inspire new projects to emerge.

Regarding the documentation of media practices, the RMA has made progress. The curious can easily find valuable information on participating media contributors to get an idea of what alternative and autonomous media looks like today. One way for the RMA to systematically record its own history would be to collaborate directly on university research projects, thereby committing less time and resources to the documentation of the alternative media scene.

The lack of resources, and the diversity of themes and perspectives, in various autonomous media remain impediments to community building and represent limitations on networks. It is crucial to counteract these deficiencies by regularly organizing conferences, workshops, and cultural events where the network's identity can be reaffirmed with face-to-face encounters.

networking the networks

Pinpointing shortcomings and underlining the revolutionary potential of this new type of network can contribute to constructing more durable and adaptable autonomous media sources. If many networks, such as Indymedia or the RMA, have proven resilient to authority, it's because they have managed to pursue networking in a respectful way, based on media autonomy.

Without further effort to coordinate or launch networks, autonomous media will continue swimming in circles. Whether permanent or temporary, autonomous media networks have the potential to stand against the corporate news organizations that shape world consciousness on a daily basis. But small fish need solidarity to fool the sharks.

Small fish of different species, colours, and origins can in fact provide a true participatory alternative only when they communicate with each other in a decentralized manner. Autonomous media might never, as a well-disseminated image by Dutch artist M.C. Escher depicts, all swim in the same direction and at the same speed with enough discipline to form a battalion capable of biting the shark's tail. They will probably continue swimming in all directions, at their own speed, pursuing their autonomous agendas. The only difference today is that with renewed conscience about the importance of networking, they have the chance to become visible and active in as many waters and streams as there are autonomous media. By upsetting, influencing or bypassing the mainstream, autonomous media networks will reach wider publics from multiple communities. This is what the RMA and many other networks are pursuing—a cooperative environment with common goals that is respectful of differences.

Once networks graduate from their initiation phase, they will need to seek allies for building ever larger networks in collaboration with social movements, academics, media educators, communication unions, and independent journalists—locally, regionally, and internationally. Networking networks is what will contribute to building a communication counter-power. Networkers unite!

notes

* Some ideas in this essay have been developed in Sénécal, Michel & Frédéric Dubois. (forthcoming 2005). *Converging Media, Diverging Politics: A Political Economy of News in the United States and Canada*. Skinner, David et al. (eds). Lanham, U.K.: Lexington Books.

[1] Grassroots Radio Coalition. Published online at: http://www.grradio.org/about/index.html [accessed February 12, 2005].

[2] Deep Dish TV. Published online at: http://www.deepdishtv.org/pages/aboutus.html [accessed March 20, 2005].

[3] A very effective temporary autonomous media collaboration is the annual Homelessness Marathon, which is organized by both campus/community radio station CKUT and street newspaper *l'Itinéraire*. In subzero temperatures, a one-night studio is installed on a Montréal sidewalk. 27 community radio stations–nationwide–produce segments and rebroadcast the bilingual Marathon. Homeless people, social and housing activists, and people from various communities across Canada, via the toll-free telephone number, discuss housing issues. A third RMA member, Les Lucioles, has produced a short video of the event, addressing issues of homelessness and media cross-polination. Apart from being a successful example of participatory communication, it also shows the benefits of coordinated actions. For more information, visit: http://www.ckut.ca/homeless.html

[4] Albert, Michael. (n.d.). "What Makes Alternative Media Alternative." *Z Magazine*. Published online at: http://www.zmag.org/whatmakesalti.htm [accessed February 12, 2005].

[5] Downing, John. (2001). Radical Media: Rebellious Communication and Social Movements. Thousand Oaks, CA, U.S.: Sage.

[6] For more information on Indymedia, read: Sénécal, Michel & Frédéric Dubois. (2005). "The Alternative Media Movement in Québec's Mediascape," *Converging Media, Diverging Politics: A political Economy of News Media in the United States and Canada*, David Skinner et al. (eds.). Lanham, U.K.: Lexington Books.

web resources

AMECQ: www.amecq.ca
Deep Dish TV: www.deepdishtv.org
Democracy Now: www.democracynow.org
FEDETVC: www.fedetvc.qc.ca
Grassroots Radio Coalition: www.grradio.org
Indymedia: indymedia.org
Nadir: www.nadir.org
Pacifica: www.pacifica.org
RMA: reseaumedia.info
Tactical Media Network: www.waag.org/tmn

AFTERWORD
linking back, looking forward
by dorothy kidd

Reading this collection reminded me of another meeting of radical media practitioners. In August 1988, I participated in the World Association of Community Radio (AMARC) Conference in Nicaragua. The conference was a watershed for alternative media. Assembled in the airy Cesar Augusto Silva Convention Centre in Managua were over 350 delegates from 48 countries. The majority were Nicaraguans from the eighteen regional radio stations of CORADEP (Corporacíon de Radiodifusión del Pueblo: The Peoples' Radio-Diffusion Corporation). Smaller delegations represented Central and South American popular, educational and guerrilla radio; North American campus and community radio, European pirate and local radio, African educational and liberation radio, as well as indigenous and women's radio projects, and other alternative media activists and researchers.[1]

In his keynote speech, European communications critic, Armand Mattelart, referred to the different contexts and definitions of our radio practice. The assembly included broadcasters from at least four distinct governing structures and social change strategies. The revolutionary Marxist paradigm of using communications primarily to seize and control state power was still alive and well in Nicaragua, Cuba, and El Salvador; although none strictly followed the vertical transmission model of classical Leninism. Several delegates were there from state-subsidized services in Canada, Europe, and the U.S., as the neoliberal attack on public service broadcasting was just beginning. The majority of faith-based stations were Catholic, with a small number of Bahai-supported stations; there were no protestant fundamentalist stations, now much more numerous. Finally, there were a number of listener-sponsored stations from North America, and a handful of independent projects, whose financial support was neither from the state or corporations.

Despite these differences, Mattelart noted our common orientation, the "construction of a collective identity to build a more just society." AMARC, he suggested, was part of a long-term project of democratizing communication; all types of radical radio were working towards a constantly evolving and building practice, defining new meanings of communication and democracy, production and professional practice, and of people.

After the conference, I travelled with other media activists to some of the CORADEP radio stations around Nicaragua. We were inspired by the local participatory experiments in which new teams of peasants, youth, and musicians took the microphones to broadcast their own news, information, and music and replace canned imported news and music. The sight of bullet-pocked stations in northern Nicaragua, fresh from attacks by the U.S.-financed Contras, elicited lots of stories from around the world. In 1988, community-oriented radio was illegal in most countries: while the Nicaraguans and Salvadorans told of constant military raids, South American and European radio activists faced harassment and closure by government agencies.

Throughout an intense two weeks, we explored the common ground and the differences among us. We exchanged experiences about the form and content of community-oriented radio, how to make programming better fit the experiences, culture, and conditions of the communities we lived in, and how to keep these projects alive in hostile media landscapes dominated by corporate and state media systems. We talked of the continuing problems of sexism, racism, and the marginalization of indigenous peoples; and we schemed of ways to deepen our translocal and transnational links and the wider global movement for the liberation of communications. A PASSION FOR RADIO, from Montréal publisher Black Rose Books, documents many of these radio experiences.

Many years, and many miles away, this new Montréal volume feels like a digital re-mix. I can hear a lot of the same chords, lyrics and tones, as well as some decided departures in the choice of instruments and jamming patterns. Although several authors show their historical links with earlier radical media and especially radio and video work, the collection also includes practices, such as the Independent Media Centre (IMC), weblogging, and ADBUSTERS' style of culture jamming, which represent significant innovations in practice and organization. As well, while technological inventiveness and global solidarity are long-standing, the rapid pace and global reach of these innovations strikes a new chord.

All of the chapters address, as did Mattelart, the ways media activists are constantly evolving and building new practices, as part of larger movements for social justice. And in the process, redefining the larger, more abstract notions of communications, democracy, subjectivity, agency, and identity. Although the concern for challenging the dominance of corporate and state media remains, it is a much less prominent feature. The framework of these authors draws much less from Marxism, and perhaps more from the anarchist socialist tradition that radical media historian John Downing describes in his work on the IMC.[2] He notes the attention given to movements over institutions, prefigurative political activity and direct action, all of which play a role here too. In fact, these are all evident in the collection's emphasis on the day-to-day processes of making democratic communications within radical media projects.

making media, making change

In FISSURES IN THE MEDIASCAPE, Clemencia Rodriguez reviews the Spanish and English-language literature about alternative media from the 1970s and 1980s. Several of these researchers and theorists participated in the call for the New World Information and Communication Order (NWICO), at UNESCO, which, among its recommendations to change global information inequities, gave a prominent role to local small-scale media. During the debate, there was almost complete consensus among the national representatives, with two very important exceptions. The U.S. and U.K. refused to come to an agreement, and instead pulled out from UNESCO; they then shifted their efforts to winning support for neoliberal communications policies, such as the privatization of public systems of broadcasting and telecommunications, and the deregulation of corporate ownership and accountability.

Afterwards, many Latin American communications advocates suggested that alternative media act as a counter balance to media consolidation and communications, and cultural imperialism. However, they offered little systematic analysis, as Rodriguez argues, of how citizen groups and grassroots organizations could contribute to the democratization of communications. In FISSURES, Rodriguez sets out to fill in this gap, with the careful documentation of what she calls "citizen's media," and an analysis of how democratic communications happens within their practices.

radical media, radical movements

The authors in this collection address the same questions. Combining roles as researchers and media activists, they map a wide range of projects in Canada. Many of these projects, as one of the Vancouver writers, Scott Uzelman, notes, operate within the contemporary movement of movements for radical and global social change. He underscores the importance of communications in movements for "social and environmental justice, which are dependent upon the establishment and maintenance of local spaces and diffuse networks of communication through which communities are imagined, developed and mobilized for action."

Several of the authors discuss the connection between radical media and social justice movements. For David Widgington the close relationship with the activist community is a defining part of being a video activist. This link may include the short-term documentation of an action or demonstration to advance an immediate agenda, or the longer-term historical documentation of a "changing society from the perspective of those [...] actively attempting to change it." Similarly, in Andréa Schmidt's account, activist journalists at the campus/community radio station CKUT collaborate with groups fighting poverty and immigration injustices, among others. As well, homeless and low-income people provide at least 50% of the content of the street newspaper, L'ITINÉRAIRE, described by Isabelle Mailloux-Béïque.

This nexus between activism and activist media is by no means new. However, its role in the expansion of global activism has been raised to a new level. Partly as a result of the work of David Garcia, Geert Lovink and the Next Five Minutes (N5M) crew in Amsterdam, many now call it "tactical media."[3] Weblogging is only one of the new open source innovations in the contemporary activist's repertoire. Dawn Paley explains how weblogging is used to quickly circulate research and knowledge as part of the grassroots pressure to keep political processes transparent and authorities accountable. She notes this kind of tactical media use is ever more urgent during these times of "information manipulating governments" such as the Liberal government in British Columbia. Widgington and van der Zon describe video and radio tactical media uses. Activist video makers provide their work to movements for debriefing after an action, to encourage reflection and self-criticism, as evidence for effective defenses in court, to identify police infiltrators, and for witnessing human rights violations. As well, as Marian van der Zon describes, activists can use low-powered radio during demonstrations to provide updates on the "movement of police or protesters, or to broadcast locations in order to access food and other amenities."

The globalization of these links between communications networks of social justice activists, and media activists has led to some inspiring transnational collaborations. For example, Widgington describes the campaign initiated when a video shot at a bauxite mine in India, by a Toronto-based videographer, was shown in Montréal, where Alcan, the mine's major shareholder has its head office. Schmidt describes the communicative bridges created between Palestine and Iraq, Europe and North America "that compels people in one struggle to take action that supports the desire for justice and the right to self-determination of people in another. [...] In projecting words and voices from those who are seldom heard, explaining the significance, the costs and the hopes of their struggles, media activists seek to catalyze active and effective solidarity movements in their countries of origin."

the tools of choice for social change

This leap forward in local and global media collaborations is partly made possible by the inventive adaptation of new information and communications technologies. Both Paley and Langlois give a central place of mention to the free and open source software movement which allows for distributed collaboration, local adaptation and free distribution of technologies such as weblogging and open publishing. David Widgington describes the interface between old and new technologies in "global collaboration among video activists;" they share footage and finished videos using the latest inexpensive desk-top technologies, as well as the older methods of face-to-face exchange. The increased power of groups like Witness to challenge human rights abuses around the world, is partly made possible by an "arsenal of computers, imaging and editing software, satellite phones, and email in the struggle for justice." Closer to home, while the radio kits discussed by Marian van der Zon have been circulating by word of mouth and hand-to-hand around the Canadian aboriginal broadcasting communities for years, she found the do-it-yourself version on the internet.

This leap in the connective capacities of global resistance networks is partly the result of a contradiction within the global capitalist system. In his earlier research on the Vancouver IMC, Scott Uzelman drew on the autonomist Marxist work of Nick Dyer-Witheford to outline how global capitalism must constantly update the training and equipment of workers and consumers around the world. While this abundance of lower-cost, easy-to-use, media production equipment, and training is an integral part of capitalist control of global production and marketing, it has also allowed for a "series of individual and collective re-appropriations."[4] Many groups around the world have seized the possibilities for new terrains of communications relatively independent of the processes of capitalist accumulation.

After a decade of naïve idealism and some costly technical miscues and misfits in activist organizations, these authors reveal a much more sophisticated and circumspect understanding of technology. Frédéric Dubois discusses the importance of carefully assessing the needs and communications culture of the group before selecting the appropriate technologies. For example, the Grassroots Radio Network values their face-to-face annual conferences; while satellite dishes and video editing equipment are essential for the Deep Dish network.

"this is what democracy looks like"

I first heard that chant in the streets of Seattle in the demonstrations against the World Trade Organization. For me, it signifies a direct action approach in which people do not wait for their representatives to lead them, but prefigure the world they envision through their own action. It is also an important theme running through this collection. Scott Uzelman argues that the attention to "new forms of participatory and democratic communication" are what distinguish autonomous media practices from alternative media. If the latter focus on regulatory reform of the institutions, and the provision of counter-content, autonomist media activists focus on changing "the ways we communicate by encouraging participation and dialogue," and "experimenting with new forms of democratic communication that are relatively independent from corporate and government power."[5]

Uzelman describes some of the mainstays of the participatory approach, including the careful attention to breaking down authoritarian power regimes through consensual decision-making and the sharing of skills. In David Widgington's account, video activist collectives are not just content-oriented but also "take the time to discuss issues, make decisions by consensus, share skills and responsibilities, and take collective credit for their successes." These principles of sharing go beyond their immediate collectives and extend to other groups in a coalition, and to the audiences with which they discuss their work.

As a counter-point, Andréa Schmidt illustrates the problems when there is not that attention to dialogue with your audience, or other groups with whom you are working in common cause. As an independent reporter in Iraq, she and her other colleagues worked separately from the "embedded" reporters and also stayed outside of the "foreigner" enclaves. However, seldom, if ever, did the activists sending reports from the "North American and European anti-war and anti-occupation movements engage Iraqis in the process of media production. [...] They did not ask Iraqis to frame the questions, nor did they ask them about their reactions to and critiques of the reports we produced." She argues for a longer-term approach, to "promote the participation of both the intended audience and those whose voices it amplifies."

Tom Liacas also critiques the consequences of not widening the circles of participation. For him, the best part of culture jamming is the do-it-yourself participation in responding immediately to your environment and changing "things that need fixing." He contrasts this with the practice of The Media Foundation, with whom he worked in Vancouver. While they have effectively promoted the cause around the world, too often they were the only ones enabled to do the culture jamming. New recruits who wanted to participate were instead addressed as consumers, and sold the group's commodities—the magazine, poster, or website.

The insider perspective of AUTONOMOUS MEDIA: ACTIVATING RESISTANCE AND DISSENT's writers also allows them to test some of the new orthodoxies about democratic practice. For Andrea Langlois, difficulties arise in practice. In her article on open publishing, she describes how the IMC adapted this open source software to "create a free information network based on a democratic model of production and distribution [...] based on collaboration and reciprocity." Their adaptation of this new technology, as some of us from earlier generations of media activists have witnessed, by-passed the hard-wired limitations of earlier electronic communications technologies, which had privileged central control systems and professional gate-keepers. Links opened up between media activists working in different media.[6]

Nevertheless, removing the electronic gates has not removed the inequalities in access, or participation that exist off-line. Not only are many of the IMC sites regularly attacked by police and state authorities, but barraged from within by everything from the most vile racist and sexist hate messages, to the most mundane idiocies. Langlois documents how the IMC collectives have invented new software and negotiated new editorial practices to bring their commitment to fighting oppressions of gender, race, sexual orientation, class, and knowledge about technology in line with the meaning of open publishing.[7] She ends with the prefigurative comment that these discussions "provide insights as to what a democratic and participatory media environment looks like."

Isabelle Mailloux-Béique shows some other complications of democratizing communications practices and participation, amidst a mediascape still very much dominated by corporate and state logics, institutions and regimes of power. *L'ITINÉRAIRE*, the Montréal street newspaper is not, in the strictest sense, an autonomous media institution; it is funded by the government and staffed by a small team of professionals, who work with paid street vendors and volunteer "street" reporters. Amidst these real power imbalances, the non-profit paper aims to be both "participatory" and "inclusive." Daily production and distribution of the paper requires constant negotiation over "hierarchies, performance, and productivity."

For Mailloux-Béique, the paper's real contribution to democracy is allowing space in the larger public discourse for the expression of homeless or low-income people, one of the most marginalized groups in North America. The paper's writers challenge the dominant media's reliance on the expertise of a small "exclusive minority of institutionalized and professionalized "experts."[8] In the process of providing insider's "truths" about critical issues such as housing, health care, employment, and social services, the street journalists not only stretch the public discourse, but also "forge and reclaim their own identities." Some vendors also take on new roles as "important players in the street: because of their ability to listen and share with strangers."

Frédéric Dubois notes the need to carefully weigh the value of internal procedures of participation against other democratic values. In his article about the Québec Alternative Media Network (RMA), he discusses the tension between practices of "individual equality" and "democratic participation" with a network's other goals of producing and circulating social justice media content outside their own circle. His network opted for a more representational governance structure, which also allowed for more fluidity in the emergence of leaders. In their account of radical libertarian media of 1970s England, the authors of *What a way to build a railroad* describe very similar tensions, between task needs, team needs and individual needs, that need to be weighed in building democratic decision-making structures.[9]

prefiguring autonomous communications

This collection contributes to a growing literature on radical media. Combining analyses and personal reflections from the ground up, the authors courageously examine their own collective practices, refusing to accept the collective amnesia which has led to generations repeating many of the same mistakes. In carefully documenting the values of participation, reciprocity, and solidarity, they provide a glimmer, or a prefiguring of what democratic communications could look like.

The volume quite rightly focuses on radical media projects. However, many of the articles delve into the overlap with related strategies of democratizing communications within social justice movements. It is my hope that future action research widens the frame to look at the values and practices among all those working to liberate communications. Our efforts to create collective projects of autonomous communications are no longer as isolated. If the extension of the world-wide social factory, shopping mall, and satellite TV, has meant a relentless attempt of global capitalism to extend the working day 24/7 everywhere, it has also meant a growing commonality of experience.

There are many different contexts, strategies, time-tables, and commitments among us, not least of which are the deepening scourges and divisions exacerbated by multiple forms of domination. What is also evident are how practices and new regimes of autonomous communications are rising up everywhere, inside, outside, and around the back of dominant institutions and logics of communications. The creation of radical media projects and institutions, autonomous of the dominant systems, are crucial. Those efforts need also to link with national and international campaigns whose goals are the re-appropriation of communications access, rights, and representation from the existing corporate and state systems; and also to support the communications efforts of people at the grassroots in widening the discourse and the franchise, in all the nooks and crannies still open to public debate and knowledge sharing.

I now live in San Francisco, a city, like Montréal, well-known for its legacy of community organizing, international solidarity and radical media. While situated far from Washington, we are subject to the same low intensity media barrage directed internally at the people in the U.S. In this new conjuncture, I feel a greater urgency to envision a project of social change, which is more inclusive of all of the ways that people are resisting, imagining, creating, and sustaining space and time for collective communications projects, independent of the rule of capital. Another world is possible, only because there are so many everywhere who are, often at great risk, seizing the time, space, and media to make it happen. Fortunately, as this volume makes clear, it's well worth it.

notes

* This title comes from Dawn Paley, in this volume: "Re/writing : Weblogs as Autonomous Spaces."

[1] AMARC began in Montréal in 1983, at the initiation of the Québec Association of Community Radio Broadcasters, and still has an office there. In 1986, Vancouver Cooperative Radio, where I worked, sponsored the conference. Moving to Managua, Nicaragua, AMARC temporarily shifted its geographical reference outside of the dominant capitalist countries of the north, and to Latin America, the region, with the strongest legacy of alternative radio and of documentation of radical media's role in social movements and social change. Working with the full support of the revolutionary Sandinista government, which was committed to the democratization of the media system, also provided opportunities to witness some of the new participatory communications projects at the CORADEP stations.

[2] Downing, John. (2003). "The Independent Media Centre Movement and the Anarchist Socialist Tradition," *Contesting Media Power: Alternative Media in a Networked World*, Couldry, Nick & James Curran. (eds.). Lanham, U.K.: Rowman & Littlefield.

[3] Garcia, David & Geert Lovink. (1997). "The ABC of Tactical Media." Published online at: http://www.ljudmila.org/nettime/zkp4/74.htm [accessed March 26, 2005].

[4] Dyer-Witheford, Nick. (1999). *Cyber-Marx: Cycles and Circuits of Struggle in High-technology Capitalism*. Urbana and Chicago: University of Illinois Press; Uzelman, Scott. (2002). *Catalyzing Participatory Communication: Independent Media Centre And The Politics Of Direct Action*. Unpublished Master's thesis: Simon Fraser University.

[5] His argument is much more fully developed in his earlier work: *Catalyzing Participatory Communication: Independent Media Centre and the Politics of Direct Action*.

⁶ Halleck, Dee Dee. (2002). *Hand-Held Visions: The Impossible Possibilities of Community Media*. New York: Fordham University Press; Kidd, Dorothy. (2004). "From Carnival to Commons: the Global IMC Network." *Confronting Capitalism: Dispatches from a Global Movement*, Yuen, Eddie et al. (eds.). Brooklyn, N.Y., U.S.: Soft Skull Press.

⁷ See also Brooten, Lisa. (2004). "Gender and.the Independent Media Centre: How Alternative Is this Alternative?," Presentation at the International Association of Media and Communication Researchers 2004 Conference, Porto Alegre, Brazil.

⁸ See Kevin Howley's account of Halifax's Street Feat. Howley, Kevin. (2003). "A Poverty of Voices: Street Papers as Communicative Democracy," *Journalism: Theory, Practice and Criticism* Vol. 4 (3), pgs. 273-292.

⁹ Landry, Charles et al. (1985). *What a Way to Run a Railroad: An Analysis of Radical Failure*. London, U.K.: Comedia.

web resources

Communication Rights in the Information Society: www.crisinfo.norg
Next Five Minutes: www.next5minutes.org
Our Media: www.ourmedianet.org
World Association of Community Radio Broadcasters: www.amarc.org

bibliography

ALBERT, Michael. (2004). "What Makes Alternative Media Alternative?" Woods Hole, MA, U.S.: *Z Magazine*. [http://www.zmag.org/whatmakesalti.htm]

ANTLIFF, Allan (ed.). (2004). *Only A Beginning: An Anarchist Anthology*. Vancouver: A Arsenal Pulp Press.

ATTON, Chris. (2002). *Alternative Media*. London, U.K.: Sage publications.

BAGDIKIAN, Ben H. (2000). *The Media Monopoly, Sixth Edition*. Boston: Beacon Press.

BEY, Hakim. (1985). *The Temporary Autonomous Zone, Ontological Anarchy, Poetic Terrorism*. New York: Autonomedia. [http://www.flashback.se/archive/taz/]

CARDON, Dominique & Fabien GRANJON. "Peut-on se libérer des formats médiatiques? Le mouvement alter-mondialisation et Internet," *Mouvements*, No. 25, January-February 2003, pgs. 1-8. Paris: La Découverte.

CARROLL, William K. & Robert A. HACKETT. "Critical Social Movements and Media Reform," *Media Development*. January 2002. London, U.K.: WACC publication. [http://www.wacc.org.uk/modules.php?name=News&file =article&sid=1489]

COULDRY, Nick. (2000). *The Place of Media Power*. London, U.K.: Routledge.

COULDRY, Nick & James CURRAN. (2003). *Contesting Media Power: Alternative Media in a Networked World*. Lanham, U.K. : Rowman & Littlefield.

CLEAVER, Harry. (1999). *Computer-linked Social Movements and the Global Threat to Capitalism*. [http://www.eco.utexas.edu/facstaff/Cleaver/ polnet.html]

CRITICAL ART ENSEMBLE. (2001). *Digital Resistance: Explorations in Tactical Media*. Brooklyn: Autonomedia. [http://www.critical-art.net]

DELEUZE, Gilles & Felix GUATTARI. (1987). *A Thousand Plateaus: Capitalism and Schizophrenia*. London, U.K.: Athlone Press.

DOWNING, John. D.H. et al. (eds.). (2001a). *Radical Media: Rebellious Communication and Social Movements*. Thousand Oaks, CA, U.S.: Sage.

DOWNING, John D.H. (2001b). "The Seattle IMC and the Socialist Anarchist Tradition," *Global Media Policy in the New Millenium*, Marc RABOY (ed.), pgs. 1-31. Luton, U.K.: Luton University Press.

DUBOIS, Frédéric. (2005). *Médias autonomes et Internet: À l'origine d'une contre-publicité?*. Unpublished Master's thesis: Université du Québec à Montréal. [http://www.reportero.org]

DYER-WITHEFORD, Nick. (1999). *Cyber-Marx: Cycles and Circuits of Struggle in High-Technology Capitalism*. Urbana and Chicago: University of Illinois Press.

FELSKI, Rita. (1989). *Beyond Feminist Aesthetics: Feminist Literature and Social Change*. Cambridge, MA, U.S.: Harvard University Press.

FRASER, Nancy. (1992). "Rethinking the Public Sphere: A Contribution to the Critique of Actually Existing Democracy," *Habermas and the Public Sphere*, Craig CALHOUN (ed.), pgs. 119-142. Boston: MIT Press.

FREIRE, Paulo. (1993). *Pedagogy of the Oppressed*. New Revised 20th-Anniversary Edition. New York: Continuum.

GARCIA, David & Geert LOVINK. (1997). "The ABC of Tactical Media," Amsterdam: Waag. [http://www.ljudmila.org/nettime/zkp4/74.htm]

GIRARD, Bruce (ed.). (1992). *A Passion for Radio*. Montréal: Black Rose Books.

GREGORY, Sam et al. (forthcoming 2005). *Video Advocacy: Using Images and Storytelling to Create Change*. London: Pluto Press.

GUMUCIO DAGRON, Alfonso. (2001). *Making Waves - Stories of Participatory Communication for Social Change*. New York: The Rockefeller Foundation.

HACKETT, Robert. "Taking Back the Media: Notes on the Potential for a Communicative Democracy Movement," *Studies in Political Economy*, No. 63, Autumn 2000, pgs. 61-86.

HALL, Stuart. (1974). "Media Power: The Double Bind," *Journal of Communication*, Vol. 24 (4), pgs.19-26.

HALLECK, Dee Dee. (2002). *Hand-Held Visions: The Impossible Possibilities of Community Media*. New York: Fordham University Press.

HAMILTON, James. (2000). "Alternative Media: Conceptual Difficulties, Critical Possibilities," *Journal of Communication Inquiry*, Vol. 24 (4), pgs. 357-378.

HERMAN, Edward S. & Noam CHOMSKY. (2002). *Manufacturing Consent. The Political Economy of the Mass Media*. New York: Pantheon Books.

JORDAN, Tim. (2002). *Activism!: Direct Action, Hacktivism, and the Future of Society*. London, U.K.: Reaktion Books.

KEANE, John. (1991). *The Media and Democracy*. Cambridge, U.K.: Polity Press.

KIDD, Dorothy. "Losing Fear: Video and Radio Productions of Native Aymara Women in Bolivia," Women in Grassroots Communication, Effecting Global Social Change, Pilar RIAÑO (ed.), *Communication and Human Values*, Vol. 16, May 1994. London, U.K.: Sage.

KIDD, Dorothy. (2003). "Indymedia.org: A New Communications Commons," *Cyberactivism*, McCAUGHEY, Martha & Michael D. AYERS (eds.), pgs. 46-69. New York: Routledge.

KIELBOWICZ, Richard B. & Clifford SCHERER. . "The Role of the Press in the Dynamics of Social Movements," *Research in Social Movements, Conflicts, and Change*. Vol. 9, 1986, pgs. 71-96.

LANGLOIS, Andrea M. (2004). *Mediating Transgressions: The Global Justice Movement and Canadian News Media.* Unpublished Master's thesis: Concordia University. [http://ase.ath.cx/hosted/liberterre/memoire.pdf]

MATTELART, Armand & Seth SIEGELAUB (eds.). (1979). *Communication and Class Struggle,* Vol. 2. New York: International General.

McCHESNEY, Robert W. (2000). *Rich Media, Poor Democracy.* New York: The New Press.

NICHOLS, John & Robert W. McCHESNEY. (2000). *It's the Media, Stupid.* New York: Seven Stories Press.

PLANT, Sadie. (1992). *The Most Radical Gesture: The Situationist International in a Postmodern Age.* London, U.K.: Routledge.

RABOY, Marc. (1984). *Movements and Messages: Media and Radical Politics in Quebec.* Toronto: Between The Lines.

RODRIGUEZ, Clemencia. (2001). *Fissures in the Mediascape: an International Study of Citizens' Media.* Cresshill, NJ, U.S.: Hampton Press.

SÉNÉCAL, Michel. (1995). *L'espace médiatique. Les communications à l'épreuve de la démocratie.* Montréal: Liber.

SKINNER, David et al. (eds.). (forthcoming 2005). *Converging Media, Diverging Politics: A political Economy of News Media in the United States and Canada.* Lanham, U.K.: Lexington Books.

STAMM, Karl-Heinz. (1988). *Alternative Öffentlichkeit. Die Erfahrungsproduktion neuer sozialer Bewegungen.* Frankfurt/Main - New York: Campus-Verlag.

UZELMAN, Scott. (2002). *Catalyzing Participatory Communication: Independent Media Centre and the Politics of Direct Action.* Unpublished Master's thesis: Simon Fraser University. [http://ender/indymedia.org/twiki/bin/view/vancouver/historyofvanimc]

WALKER, Jesse. (2001). *Rebels on the Air: An Alternative History of Radio in America.* New York: New York University Press.

WARNER, Michael. (2002). *Publics and Counterpublics.* New York: Zone Books.

WINTER, James. (1997). *Democracy's Oxygen: How Corporations Control the News.* Montréal: Black Rose Books.

WHITE, Robert A. (1995). "Democratization of Communication as a Social Movement Process," *The Democratization of Communication,* Philip LEE (ed.). Cardiff, U.K.: University of Wales Press.

YUEN, Eddie et al. (eds). *Confronting Capitalism: Dispatches from a Global Movement.* Brooklyn, N.Y., U.S.: Soft Skull Press.

ZIMMERMANN, Patricia R. (2000). *States of Emergency: Documentaries, Wars, Democracies.* Minneapolis: University of Minnesota Press.

contributors

bernard bastien works as a professional software designer and has always been interested in electronic music, radio communication, journalism, and photography. After ten years of sporadic and unsatisfying photography, the planets aligned for him the day the Summit of the Americas moved into his backyard, in Québec City, in April 2001. There, he found great images to capture, new ideas, humanism, talented people, and true dreams for a better world. In meeting passionate photographers, he realized photography's potential for accomplishing its contemplative nature and its sense of witnessing. The Summit made him discover the Indymedia network and many organizations involved in the promotion of alternative systems through popular education and mobilization. He joined the first to help with the second. See his web site at www.neonyme.net

frédéric dubois is a media activist and independent journalist. He holds a Bachelors of Commerce from McGill University and a Masters in Communications from Université du Québec à Montréal. Frédéric has spent many months off-the-beaten-track, living, traveling, and writing in the Americas, Europe, and India. A backpacker since childhood, Frédéric continues to cross borders in pursuit of grassroots accounts and hidden stories. He has taken part in several media projects such as CMAQ (Québec Indymedia) and wrote his thesis on autonomous media and the internet.

fanchon esquieu studied Applied Arts in Paris and further pursued landscape architecture. In 2001, she discovered Montréal and decided to let down an anchor. She is fascinated by the energy and colour of the city, which gives her the needed energy to translate this onto paper and canvas. Between art and landscapes, through lines and vivid colours, she communicates her vision of the world. With her drawings, she tells the story of those she meets. Between 2002 and 2004, she made illustrations for benefit concerts, alternative magazines, and CMAQ (Québec Indymedia), and organized exhibitions in gallery-bars. Some of her work can be found on the Jivaros artists' collective website. See www.jivaros.org

élise gravel completed a graphic design program in Montréal, then chose illustration as the focus of her productive career. As an illustrator, she provides services for various sectors but always makes time for social causes in line with her values. Élise has written and illustrated several children's books and hopes to produce many more in the coming years. For more info, see her website: www.elisegravel.com

dorothy kidd has worked in alternative media since the early 1970s, including: community video in Toronto, community radio in Vancouver, aboriginal radio and television with the Okalagatiget Communications Society in northern Labrador, the Inuit Broadcasting Corporation and the Wawatay Aboriginal Communications Society in northern Ontario, and feminist presses in Vancouver, Toronto, and Winnipeg.

Dorothy's overall research agenda includes mapping the historical development of a transnational communications liberation movement. Current research projects include the documentation of the use of communications by counter-publics and alternative media in San Francisco; the U.S. media reform movement, and their transnational counterparts. She is actively involved in the work of Media Alliance in San Francisco, and the international Our Media network. She teaches Media Studies at the University of San Francisco.

andrea langlois holds a BA in Women's Studies and Professional Writing from the University of Victoria, and recently finished her Masters in Media Studies at Concordia University in Montréal. Driven by a need to understand why media are imperative to social movements, she has spent the past few years studying and deconstructing the relationship between social movements and mass media. In her activist life, she has been involved in feminist and queer groups, and autonomous media projects ranging from culture jamming to Indymedia and community radio. Her favourite tools of resistance are stickers, her laptop, and her voice.

tom liacas' life as an activist began when he got involved with ADBUSTERS, eventually becoming their campaigns manager. He helped found a local culture jamming collective in Vancouver during that period. He later went to Montréal to rethink his strategy and continued to dabble in jamming while doing his MA in Communications. He has worked with friends in Slovenia to help develop the international Festival of Radical Communications. Now mellower and a new dad, he works on progressive social change projects for more benign and docile clients.

isabelle mailloux-béïque has been a volunteer and active member of CMAQ (Québec Indymedia) since 2001. Her work focuses primarily on promoting her local independent media centre as an alternative source of information and a tool to becoming the media. She also participates in the collective effort by organizing and producing information for their website. Masters candidate in Communications at Université de Montréal, she is investigating alternative communication practices. She's particularly interested in the Montréal street newspaper, L'ITINÉRAIRE, and principally in the practices of media production by street journalists. Isabelle works as a research and teacher's assistant at her university.

dawn paley is a social justice activist and writer from Ruskin, British Columbia. Many hours of her life have been happily devoted to political and grassroots organizing. In 2003, she graduated from Simon Fraser University with a Bachelor's degree in Women's Studies and First Nations' Studies. Since then, she's worked as a journalist and photographer in South Africa and Latin America, trying to bring marginalized voices to the fore through her work. At any given time, Dawn may be spotted doing the following dance moves: the windmill, the motorcycle, the scissors, or the shopping cart. She likes banana slugs, haikus, mail art, and playing ultimate Frisbee. Dawn's kept a weblog since early 2002.

chester rhoder was born in the Eastern Townships of Québec and is a farm boy at heart. He is the founder of Typo-pawsitive where he designs books and activist art from his barnyard studio. He is well known for climbing trees and running circles around the competition.

andréa schmidt lives, works, and organizes in Montréal. She participates in a number of local anti-imperialist and anti-capitalist projects and solidarity groups in a small effort to proliferate resistance to the systems of domination that organize the globe. She also sits on the board of the Institute for Anarchist Studies, and co-edits the IAS's bi-annual magazine, PERSPECTIVES ON ANARCHIST THEORY. Andréa reported from occupied Iraq from February to May 2004, where she visited as a delegate of the Iraq Solidarity Project. Her written dispatches are available on-line at www.en-camino.org.

scott uzelman is a PhD candidate and Social Sciences and Humanities Research Council of Canada Doctoral Fellow in the Joint Programme in Communication and Culture at York University where he is currently studying the logic of direct action in struggles for social and environmental justice. He has been involved in the media democracy movement for several years as a researcher with NewsWatch Canada at Simon Fraser University (SFU) and as a founding member of the Vancouver Chapter of the Campaign for Press and Broadcasting Freedom. In 2002, he completed a MA thesis at SFU on participatory research he conducted with fellow media activists in establishing and developing the Vancouver Independent Media Centre.

marian van der zon is a multi-disciplinary artist who delves into sound art, sound documentary, writing and spoken word performance. She has a background in Women's Studies and recently finished a Master's degree in Media Studies at Concordia University. Marian's interests are varied, but often return to an examination of voice, morality, and women's issues. Marian hosted and contributed to Victoria radio station CFUV's STIRFRY (VIPIRG) for several years, and produced pieces for Montréal's CKUT, and CBC radio in Victoria. She continues to experiment with low wattage transmitters, broadcasting through Temporary Autonomous Radio and encouraging radio karaoke. When she is not dabbling with the musical styling of Victoria basement bands Tailgate Party or Five Year Plan, she is usually found wandering the mountains of British Columbia.

david widgington is a full-time media activist and a part-time cheap labourer. He is a founding member of the Montréal-based video activist collective Les Lucioles and a volunteer member of campus/community radio station CKUT 90.3FM, where he has teched, hosted, and produced a weekly two-hour morning show. He started small-time publishing in 1998 as publisher of Cumulus Press. His BA in Geography has motivated—and was motivated by—railway travel on four continents, and has helped him never get lost longer than necessary.

acknowledgements

First and foremost, we would like to thank all of the authors who put their ideas and experiences on paper for us, and the artists and photographers who helped illustrate the creative aspects of autonomous media.

Thank you to David Widgington, our publisher, for helping us realize our vision, to Chester Rhoder for designing the book, and to the Chan Clan, Simon Pierre, and *les décorateurs engagéEs* for inspiration and motivation. We would also like to acknowledge the help of Clara Gabriel who revised the texts written by francophones and engaged in lengthy discussions about language and style.

Thank you to all the activists whose work and dedication inspires us, especially: Abhi, Aziz, Barbara, Bruno, Cat-minoune, Dexter, Francis, Gretchen, Geneviève, Jenn, Josée, Julien, Manu, Marie-Ève, Martin, Patrick, Roberto, Samira, Sarita, Stefan, Stéphane, Tamara, all those at CMAQ and CKUT.

To the profs who encouraged our interest in radical media: Martin Allor, Isabelle Gusse, Yasmin Jiwani, Dorothy Kidd, Monika Kin Gagnon, Chantal Nadeau, Serge Proulx, Marc Raboy, Leslie Regan Shade, Michel Sénécal, and David Skinner.

Respect and appreciation for the work and kindness of Nick Couldry, John Downing, Naomi Klein, and Clemencia Rodriguez.

To our families and friends for supporting and encouraging us in everything we do.

And those closest to us during this process, Dawn and Mélanie, who travelled the Andean cordillera with frenetic editors at their side.

Thank you.

Andrea Langlois & Frédéric Dubois

p.s., comments are welcome: www.cumuluspress.com